Lejourne

QUICK
CUISINE

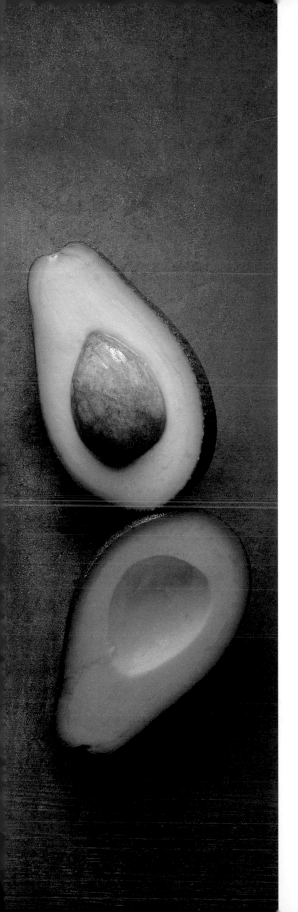

QUICK
CUISINE

LEWIS ESSON
with HENRIETTA GREEN & MARIE-PIERRE MOINE

Conran Octopus

DEDICATION

To Colin Clark and Colin MacIvor
for their inspiration
and to Ajit

Throughout the book, recipes are for four people
unless otherwise stated.

Editorial Direction: Lewis Esson Publishing
Design: Sue Storey
Photography: Patrice de Villiers
Illustrations: Lynne Robinson
Food for Photography: Janey Suthering
Styling: Penny Markham
Editorial Assistant: Penny David
Production: Sonya Sibbons

First published in 1991 by Shelton Books,
a division of Conran Octopus Limited,
37 Shelton Street, London WC2H 9HN

This edition published in 1992 by
Conran Octopus Limited

Text copyright © Lewis Esson, Henrietta Green and
Marie-Pierre Moine

British Library Cataloguing-in-Publication Data

Esson, Lewis
 Quick cuisine : sensational food in less than
 30 minutes.
 I. Title II. Green, Henrietta III. Moine,
 Marie-Pierre
 641.555

ISBN 1-85029-436-4

Typeset by Servis Filmsetting Ltd
Printed and bound by
Kim Hup Lee Printing Co PTE Ltd, Singapore

CONTENTS

INTRODUCTION

This is a book for food lovers in a hurry – people who enjoy cooking and eating at home, but don't usually have much time to spend in the kitchen.

The secret of Quick Cuisine lies in turning lack of time into an advantage. As with chefs in fashionable restaurants who create great dishes in minutes, the skill is knowing exactly what can be achieved in the time. Slowly simmered delicate combinations are out – instead bold fresh flavours, natural textures and exciting combinations are the order of the day.

Quick Cuisine's approach is based on using the best possible fresh produce available. Quality ingredients are a must – since there is no time to nurture or disguise them, they will have to give of their best immediately.

The equipment required is straightforward, as found in most domestic kitchens, so there is no need to assemble a great batterie de cuisine to cook from this book. However, a good food processor, an efficient grill, a large sturdy frying pan, a sharp knife and a sturdy pair of scissors are all essential.

Preparation and cooking techniques are simple, if not obvious! The Quick Cook has to be prepared to be bold and use his or her hands for shredding or tearing leaves or for patting seasonings into food, for instance; to use eyes and instincts to judge weights and measures, and to exercise simple common sense and basic initiative at all times.

This hands-on approach of Quick Cuisine is fun and unpretentious. If you have previously been put off by the long lists of ingredients and finicky methods of traditional cooking, Quick Cuisine will make a confident cook out of you in no time at all.

1

THE QUICK APPROACH

The secret of Quick Cuisine lies in a very simple three-fold approach: buying the right ingredients; using labour-saving equipment and employing time-saving techniques.

As Quick Cuisine makes the most of the natural full flavours of food, the ingredients must be truly fresh and of the best quality. It also takes advantage of today's wide range of ready-prepared food, from trimmed and washed salad leaves to filleted fish and jointed poultry: the extra cost is more than justified by the time saved.

Apart from the essential food processor, the equipment we use is neither extravagant nor complex. Simple utensils, such as graters, zesters, good knives and scissors and versatile woks, make possible many of the speedy preparation and cooking techniques we use.

These techniques are simplicity itself, to ensure the greatest effect with the minimum of effort: from straightforward short-cuts, like tearing ingredients or snipping them with scissors straight into the pan, to the correct way to grill or sauté for speed and effectiveness.

BUYING the BEST INGREDIENTS

- Buy the freshest food you can find.

- Buy 'little and often' – even items such as spices!

- Make the most of seasonal produce.

- Buy from reliable suppliers where freshness and quality are guaranteed.

- Where appropriate, make use of convenience packs of prepared food: boned and trimmed meat, skinned and filleted fish, washed, trimmed and cut vegetables and salad leaves, etc.

- Use fresh herbs for more potent flavours. Grow them in pots on the kitchen windowsill or stand cut bunches in water in a shady place. Cut herbs also keep well wrapped in damp newspaper inside a plastic bag in the refrigerator. Generally in this sort of speedy cooking, dried herbs don't have time to develop their full flavour.

- Use best quality extra-virgin olive oil for salad dressings and for cooking. However, a mixture of equal parts olive oil and sunflower oil is more economical for cooking and has a less intrusive flavour which may sometimes be critical.

- Unsalted or low-salt butter allows you to adjust the seasoning yourself, especially in flavoured butters with salty ingredients such as anchovies or cheese, and it is essential when making sweet butter sauces.

- Use the same wine in cooking as you drink – so-called 'cooking wines' can ruin a dish.

- Use wine or cider vinegar rather than malt for a better, more subtle flavour.

- Use freshly ground black pepper for greater pungency.

- Use sea salt as it brings out the flavour of food more powerfully and you'll need less – especially if you use a salt mill.

- Try to buy uncoated lemons and oranges if you are going to use the zest. If you can only get waxed fruit, scrub them thoroughly in hot soapy water, rinse well and pat dry.

- TRY TO KEEP THE FOLLOWING STAPLES IN THE LARDER:

loaf of good bread
half dozen eggs
head of garlic
packet of sea salt
packet of black peppercorns
packet of caster sugar

- ALWAYS HAVE THE FOLLOWING ESSENTIALS
IN THE REFRIGERATOR:

575 ml/1 pt milk
225 g/½ lb unsalted butter
2 or 3 lemons
1 or 2 oranges (or some fresh orange juice)
bunch of spring onions
bottle of dry white wine
225 g/½ lb unsmoked streaky bacon
300 ml/½ pt carton of yoghurt
300 ml/½ pt carton of double cream, crème
    fraîche or fromage frais
115 g/4 oz chunk of Parmesan cheese
jar of good made mustard
½ bottle dry sherry

- KEEP THE FOLLOWING FOR BACK-UP IN
THE FREEZER:

another loaf of good bread
packet of muffins
225 g/½ lb butter
225 g/½ lb packet of leaf spinach
115 g/4 oz packet of small garden peas
1 l/1¾ pt good vanilla ice-cream
1.1 l/2 pt chicken stock
ice cubes

● STOCK YOUR STORE-CUPBOARD WITH THE FOLLOWING:

450 g / 1 lb packet of 10-minute rice
450 g / 1 lb dried pasta
450 g / 1 lb easy-cook Chinese noodles
sachet of court-bouillon
bottle of extra-virgin olive oil
bottle of sunflower oil
small can or bottle of walnut oil
small bottle of chilli oil
bottle of red wine, white wine or cider vinegar
small bottle of sherry vinegar
small bottle of balsamic vinegar
bottle of soy sauce
tin of English mustard powder
tin of five-spice powder
large bottle of Worcestershire sauce
tube or bottle of anchovy essence or paste (keep in refrigerator once opened)
tube of tomato paste (keep in refrigerator once opened)
bottle of Tabasco sauce
bottle of harissa or chilli sauce
packet of whole nutmegs
drum of paprika
packet of cumin seeds
packet of small dried chillis
jar of sun-dried tomatoes in oil
jar of capers
packet of soft brown sugar
packet of icing sugar
jar of clear honey
jar of redcurrant jelly
jar of good marmalade
packet of blanched almonds
packet of seedless raisins
packet of pine nuts
packet of walnuts
packet of hazelnuts
packets of poppy and sesame seeds

● KEEP THE FOLLOWING FOOD IN CANS:

clams in brine
tuna fish in oil
anchovy fillets in oil
artichoke hearts
cannellini beans
chick peas
flageolets
sweetcorn kernels
red sweet peppers
chopped tomatoes

● A well-stocked drinks cabinet is an asset in this sort of cooking. Essentials include vermouth, rum, whisky, brandy and cassis. Cider is also very useful but, like sherry, should be kept in the refrigerator. Alternatively, buy it in cans. Unlike wine, it is quite acceptable to cook with an inferior brand of spirits, such as brandy or rum, in order to save the better brands for drinking. Many off-licences and supermarkets stock a wide range of miniatures of brandies and liqueurs which are very handy for cooking.

LABOUR-SAVING KITCHEN EQUIPMENT

• Most quick cooking depends on a good food processor. If you don't already have one, buy one of the new designs with a detachable small bowl within the main bowl for chopping small amounts. Give the machine a permanent place out on the worktop so you don't have to heft it out of a cupboard each time you want to use it.

• Good chef's knives save time. Have at least 3 in different sizes, and sharpen them regularly. Also buy a small stainless-steel fruit knife with a serrated edge. Keep knives in a handy place so they are always within easy reach.

• Have a couple of good pairs of all-purpose kitchen scissors and keep them sharp. They are useful for everything from jointing poultry to snipping herbs.

• A lemon zester allows you to pare off strips of peel from citrus fruit without bringing up the bitter pith underneath.

• Have several good large sturdy chopping boards. Keep one exclusively for preparing raw meats.

• A good stout pastry or paint brush is useful for applying oil to food, but avoid nylon bristles as they may melt on contact with hot food.

• A salad spinner gets leaves really dry and saves a lot of time otherwise spent patting them.

• A wok is essential for stir-frying. Get one with a matching scoop to stir the food with. The single-handled versions are easier to manoeuvre. Buy the very basic and inexpensive ones from Chinese supermarkets which may be replaced readily.

• A good quality sauté pan is worth the investment. Make sure the base is thick and heavy, for even browning, and that the sides are quite high, so that the food can be stirred vigorously and liquid ingredients added later. It should also come with a tight-fitting lid for subsequent slower cooking after the initial browning.

• A proper pasta pan, tall with an inner basket so that the pasta may be lifted from the water with ease, is expensive but it will pay for itself many times over.

• Try to have one or two frying-pans in different sizes, to match the type and quantity of food being cooked. Non-stick pans are best as they permit healthy dry-frying. A small omelette pan is also very useful.

TIME-SAVING TECHNIQUES

• Snip herbs and leaves with scissors directly into pans or salad bowls rather than chopping them on boards. Firm fruit and food such as chicken livers, mushrooms and sliced cooked meats can also be snipped.

• Tear or shred food like salad leaves or cooked chicken into bowls or pans. This is not only quicker than chopping, but gives a better texture and keeps more of their juices.

• Wherever possible, crumble and flake foods like cheese and cooked fish into pans and bowls rather than taking the time to chop them.

• Many foods, including firmer vegetables as well as cheese, can be grated instead of finely chopped. For larger quantities, do it in the food processor.

• Our phrase 'whizz in the food processor' means processing just long enough to achieve the desired texture. It is usually necessary first to break the food into manageable pieces so the machine can deal with them efficiently. When whizzing, be careful not to over-process foods as they can easily become a textureless mush.

• Quick cuisine makes a great deal of use of the zest of citrus fruits. Use only uncoated or well scrubbed fruit. Grate the zest with the fine section of a grater or pare it with a zester. Either way, try not to press too hard so as not to bring up too much of the bitter pith underneath the peel.

• A quick and easy means of flavouring with garlic is to halve a clove and rub it over the bottom of a pan or bowl or even smear it directly over firm food. Otherwise, crush cloves with the side of a wide knife or use a garlic press.

• As Quick Cuisine does not really allow the time for marinating, we make much use of flavoured pastes and crusts when grilling, pan-frying or baking. The pastes are usually bound with oil to ensure that they stick to the food during cooking. Paint them on with a stout brush, spread them on with a spatula or simply press them on with your hands.

• For those dishes which require boiling water, to speed things up heat the water in a kettle. For dishes like pasta, when you need a large amount of water, heat some in the kettle and the rest in the pan.

• Most meat needs to be seared in the early stages of cooking to seal in its juices and give it a good colour. Don't be afraid of using high temperatures to achieve this as rapidly as possible.

• When grilling, turn on the grill as early as possible so that it has the time to get properly heated while you are preparing the ingredients. Try to use only uniformly thin pieces of food for quick and even cooking.

● Sautéing is a very useful technique in Quick Cuisine. The main ingredients, usually cut in small pieces, are initially cooked in butter or oil, with frequent stirring, over a high heat to brown and seal them. Flavourings, such as wine and herbs, are then added and the dish simmered gently for a few minutes to finish the cooking.

● Stir-frying is similar to sautéing, but is done in a wok. The food is again usually cut into strips or small pieces and is kept on the move all the time over quite a high heat. The shape of the wok allows cooked food to be shoved to the cooler top of the rim while new ingredients are cooked in the hotter base.

● Liquids, especially sauces, are often reduced to intensify their flavours and thicken them to a required consistency. They are simply boiled rapidly for as long as is necessary. The wider the pan, the faster the liquid will boil off, but if the pan is too wide it can be difficult to control the process.

● After food has been pan-fried or grilled, the pan is usually deglazed with a little liquid, usually water, stock, vinegar, lemon juice, wine or other alcohol. Stirring the liquid over the heat with a wooden spoon and scraping up the sediment gets all the flavour from the base of the pan to make a good sauce or gravy.

2

SOUPS

Soups provide an interesting and substantial first course without a great deal of effort. Armed with a food processor, all of these soups are very easy to make, especially the no-cook variety.

The secret of our soups lies in freshness and the quick release of flavours rather than long simmering. Many can simply be made with water, but a few call for stock and for this purpose a stock-cube will not do. Use a good home-made stock or one of the new brands of ready-made stock available in bottles or tubs.

Many of these soups also make the most satisfying of light meals on their own, served with crusty bread or one of our 'tartinis' (see pages 32–6) and perhaps followed by a salad or fruit and cheese.

Left: Prawn Bisque (page 23); right: Quick Soup au Pistou (page 22)

NO-COOK SOUPS

These cold soups need no cooking and are incredibly quick to prepare. If the ingredients are cold enough the soups can simply be served as they are. For a chilled soup, add some ice cubes to the serving bowls or whizz them first in the food processor as the soup is made.

COLD CREAM of TOMATO SOUP with CHERVIL

🕐 *under 10 minutes*

If the tomatoes are really sweet there is no need for the sugar.

450 g / 1 lb ripe tomatoes
1 tsp sugar
bunch of fresh chervil
150 ml / $\frac{1}{4}$ pt single cream
salt and pepper

1   Whizz the tomatoes with the sugar in the food processor until they become light and frothy, snipping in half the chervil with the machine still running.

2   Pour into a large bowl and mix in just enough cream to give a thick but runny consistency. Season to taste with salt and pepper.

3   Pour into individual bowls and snip the remaining chervil over the top of each bowl. Drop a few ice cubes in each bowl, if wished.

COLD AVOCADO, SPINACH and SPRING ONION SOUP

🕐 *under 10 minutes*

Use only perfectly ripe avocados for this dish. Pick over the spinach leaves and trim off any thick stems, or buy packs of ready-washed and trimmed leaves.

2 large ripe avocados
1 lime
4 spring onions
450 g / 1 lb baby spinach leaves
575 ml / 1 pt vegetable or chicken stock or water
dash of Worcestershire sauce
pinch of cayenne
salt and pepper

1   Halve, peel and stone the avocados and then coarsely chop the flesh. Squeeze the juice from the lime and pour a little over the avocado. Snip the spring onions into short lengths.

2   In the food processor, whizz until smooth the avocados and spring onions with the remaining lime juice and almost all the spinach leaves. Whizz in a little stock or water.

3   Pour into a large bowl and add just enough stock or water to get a thick but runny consistency.

4   Season to taste with Worcestershire sauce, cayenne and salt and pepper.

5   Pour into individual bowls and add a few ice cubes to each if you wish. Garnish with a few finely snipped spinach leaves.

COLD FRESH HERB SOUP

🕐 *under 20 minutes*

You do need a good quality stock for this soup. Use any one of the herbs on their own or a mixture as preferred, depending on availability. Rocket, sorrel and purslane are also good in this dish.

1 l / 1$\frac{3}{4}$ pt vegetable or chicken stock
3 or 4 small handfuls of fresh herbs, including flat-leaf parsley, lemon thyme, basil and tarragon
200 ml / 7 fl oz sour cream
salt and pepper

1   Whizz a little stock or water in the food processor with most of the herbs until they are well chopped.

2   Add all but 4 tablespoons of the cream and blend lightly, then pour into a tureen or large bowl. Stir in just enough of the remaining stock or water to give a good thick but runny consistency.

3   Season the soup to taste and then pour into individual bowls.

4   Swirl the reserved cream on the tops of the bowls and garnish with a few herb sprigs.

Cold Fresh Herb Soup

● HOT SOUPS

The good fresh flavours of the ingredients are strong enough to allow these soups to be made using only water instead of stock. Time can be saved by heating the water in a kettle while processing the vegetables. Many of these soups are substantial enough to make good snack meals, served with crusty bread.

QUICK SOUPE au PISTOU

🕐 *under 20 minutes*

The pistou sauce for this version of a classic Provençal soup has many other uses and is particularly good with firm-fleshed fish, poultry and steamed vegetables. It also makes a good pasta sauce.

1.1 1/2 pt of vegetable or chicken stock or water
400 g / 14 oz ripe tomatoes
150 ml / $\frac{1}{4}$ pt olive oil
4 spring onions
450 g / 1 lb French beans
1 large courgette
450 g / 1 lb canned red haricot or kidney beans
170 g / 6 oz vermicelli
for the pistou:
5 garlic cloves
bunch of fresh basil leaves
55 g / 2 oz Parmesan
55 g / 2 oz Gruyère or Emmental

1 Put the stock or water to heat and coarsely chop the tomatoes.

2 Put one third of the oil in a large heavy-bottomed saucepan and place over a moderate heat. Snip in the spring onions and cook for a minute or two.

3 Add the tomatoes to the pan and cook for another few minutes while preparing the other vegetables.

4 Top and tail the French beans and snip them into short lengths. Slice the courgette.

5 Add the boiling stock or water to the pan followed by the prepared vegetables, the drained canned beans and the vermicelli. Simmer gently for about 10 minutes.

6 Meanwhile, make the pistou: peel the garlic cloves and put them in the food processor with the basil and half the Parmesan in pieces. Whizz to a coarse paste and then, with the machine still running, add the remaining oil in a steady stream. Season with salt and pepper.

7 Season the soup to taste and stir in the pistou just before serving.

8 Grate the remaining Parmesan and Gruyère or Emmental and serve it separately, for sprinkling on the soup.

PEA and SMOKED HAM SOUP

🕐 *under 10 minutes*

1.1 1/2 pt vegetable or chicken stock or water
30 g / 1 oz butter
4 spring onions
450 g / 1 lb frozen peas
1 or 2 sprigs of summer savory
300 ml / $\frac{1}{2}$ pt thick yoghurt
2 thick slices of smoked ham
small bunch of chives
salt and pepper

1 Put the stock or water to heat.

2 Melt the butter in a large heavy-bottomed saucepan over a moderate heat and snip in the spring onions. Sauté for a minute or two.

3 Add the peas and savory with a little of the stock or water and bring to the boil, then simmer for a minute or two.

4 Whizz the mixture in the food processor until smooth. Return to the pan.

5 Mix in the yoghurt and just enough of the stock to give a good thick but runny consistency. Season with pepper and a little salt if necessary.

6 Pour into bowls and snip over the ham and chives.

PRAWN BISQUE

🕐 *under 20 minutes*

1.1 1/2 pt fish stock
1 fennel bulb
450 g / 1 lb cooked peeled prawns
25 g / $\frac{3}{4}$ oz butter
4 spring onions
handful of parsley
1 bay leaf
150 ml / $\frac{1}{4}$ pt dry white wine
juice of 1 lemon
300 ml / $\frac{1}{2}$ pt whipping cream
1 tbsp brandy
salt and cayenne pepper

1   Put the stock to heat. Remove the outer leaves and woody core from the fennel and chop it into small pieces, reserving the feathery leaves. Halve all but 12 small prawns.

2   Melt the butter in a large heavy-bottomed saucepan over a moderate heat. Add the fennel to the pan and then snip in the spring onions and parsley with its stalks. Sauté for about 3 minutes.

3   Add the bay leaf, wine and lemon juice. Cook rapidly until syrupy. Remove the bay leaf and add the halved prawns. Stir well and pour in a little of the boiling stock. Simmer for 2 or 3 minutes.

4   Whizz the mixture in the food processor. Return the mixture to the pan, stir in the rest of the stock and add the cream and brandy.

5   Season to taste with cayenne and salt and heat gently for a minute or two. Garnish with the reserved prawns and snip over the fennel fronds.

Variation:
If the prawns don't have much colour and the soup is very pale, add some tomato paste.

SWEET-AND-SOUR NOODLE SOUP

🕐 *under 10 minutes*

Try any one of the wide variety of noodles now available in larger supermarkets as well as Oriental food shops. If you use those which need only soaking, time may be saved in the final simmering.

1.1 1/2 pt vegetable or chicken stock or water
4 slices of rindless maple-cure bacon
piece of fresh ginger about 2.5 cm / 1 in thick
3 spring onions
2 garlic cloves
1 tbsp sugar
pinch of five-spice powder
115 g / 4 oz oyster mushrooms
1 Chinese cabbage or cos lettuce
1 tbsp soy sauce
2 tbsp vinegar
115 g / 4 oz thread noodles
1 tbsp sesame oil
salt and pepper

1   Put the stock to heat.

2   Put a large heavy-bottomed saucepan over a high heat and snip in the bacon. Dry-fry for a minute or two.

3   Meanwhile peel the ginger and put it in the food processor. Add the spring onions, broken into pieces, followed by the garlic. Process to a paste and add to the pan along with the sugar and five-spice powder. Stir-fry for 1 minute.

4   Roughly chop the mushrooms and leaves and add to the pan with the soy sauce. Stir-fry for 1 minute.

5   Pour in the boiling stock and the vinegar, break in the noodles and simmer for a few minutes.

6   Season to taste with salt and pepper, pour into individual bowls and dribble a few drops of sesame oil over each.

CHICKEN and LEEK SOUP

🕐 *under 15 minutes*

1.1 1/2 pt vegetable or chicken stock or water
25 g/$\frac{3}{4}$ oz butter
2 sun-dried tomatoes in oil
4 spring onions
1 stalk of celery
115 g/4 oz skinned boneless chicken breast
2 leeks
150 ml/$\frac{1}{4}$ pt dry white wine
small bunch of parsley
salt and pepper

1 Put the stock or water to heat.

2 Melt the butter with 1 tablespoon of the oil from the sun-dried tomatoes over a moderate heat in a large heavy-bottomed saucepan. Snip in the spring onions and the celery and cook for 2 or 3 minutes.

3 Meanwhile slice or shred the chicken into small strips and snip the sun-dried tomatoes. Trim and halve the leeks and rinse them under running water to free them of any grit.

4 Add the chicken and sun-dried tomatoes to the pan, increase the heat slightly and sauté for 2 minutes, stirring frequently.

5 Shake off any excess moisture from the leeks and then snip them coarsely into the pan.

6 Sauté the contents of the pan until the leeks have just wilted.

7 Pour in the boiling stock or water and the wine and simmer gently for about 5 minutes.

8 Season to taste, pour into warmed bowls and snip over some parsley to serve.

POACHED SMOKED HADDOCK and EGG SOUP with MILK

🕐 *under 10 minutes*

Use only best quality undyed smoked haddock. You can also try poaching the eggs whole in the soup, until they are just set but still runny inside.

450 g/1 lb smoked haddock
1 1/1$\frac{3}{4}$ pt full-fat milk
2 bay leaves
4 black peppercorns
4 eggs
1 tbsp horseradish sauce
pinch of cayenne
pepper

1 Put the fish in a pan and cover with the milk. Add the bay leaves and whole peppercorns. Bring to the boil and simmer gently for about 5 minutes.

2 Remove the fish from the pan and allow it to cool slightly. Remove the skin and flake the flesh into the food processor.

3 Strain the milk and add a few spoonfuls to the fish. Whizz briefly to a coarse mixture, but do not over-process.

4 Put this mixture in a large saucepan and stir in the remaining strained milk. Bring to the boil over a moderate heat and then reduce the heat to a simmer.

5 Beat the eggs lightly and stir them into the liquid with the horseradish sauce. Simmer for 2 or 3 minutes and then season to taste with pepper.

6 Pour into bowls and sprinkle each lightly with cayenne to serve.

CANNELLINI BEAN, GARLIC and CURLY ENDIVE SOUP

🕐 *under 10 minutes*

1 1/1$\frac{3}{4}$ pt vegetable or chicken stock
5 tbsp olive oil
3 garlic cloves
1 small head of curly endive (frisée)
1 can (425 g/15 oz) of cannellini beans
salt and pepper

1 Put the stock to heat.

2 Heat half the oil in a large heavy-bottomed saucepan over a moderate heat and then crush in the garlic. Sauté for about 3 minutes.

3 Meanwhile snip the endive leaves into small pieces and drain the beans.

4 Add the endive shreds to the pan, reserving a few, and cook gently until the leaves are just wilted, then add the beans.

5 Stir in the boiling stock and bring back to the boil. Simmer gently for about 5 minutes.

6 Adjust the seasoning. Just before serving, trickle in the remaining oil and finely snip over some reserved endive leaves.

Cannellini Bean, Garlic and Curly Endive Soup

3

STARTERS, SNACKS and LIGHT MEALS

There are in this chapter dozens of interesting recipes for first courses or snack lunches which are very simple to make either in the middle of a busy day or while preparing a main course. Cooking most of them takes no longer than reheating an expensive ready-cooked convenience meal.

Many people today are turning to meals which consist of two starters or light dishes and most of ours are also easily scaled up to make substantial main courses in their own right. As a rule of thumb, just double the ingredients. In the egg dishes, for instance, use two eggs per person, rather than one.

Pasta is particularly versatile, easily adjusted for small or large numbers, and makes a fine supper-party main course when served with a large salad.

Left: Grilled Radicchio with Goats' Cheese (page 28); right: rigatoni with Poached Baby Vegetables (page 42)

BRESAOLA with SHAVED PARMESAN and OLIVE OIL

🕐 *under 10 minutes*

Scandinavian cheese slicers, with angled cutting slots, are useful for cutting firm cheese into thin shavings.

55 g / 2 oz chunk of parmesan
6 tbsp extra-virgin olive oil
1 tbsp lemon juice
12 thin slices of bresaola
small bunch of flat-leaf parsley
pepper

1   Cut the cheese into thin slivers. Mix the oil and lemon juice in a bowl and season with pepper.

2   Arrange 3 slices of bresaola on each plate and pour the dressing over them.

3   Place 2 or 3 slivers of cheese over the meat on each plate.

4   Season with some more pepper and snip over the parsley.

CARROTS VINAIGRETTE

🕐 *under 10 minutes*

Use baby carrots if available, otherwise coarsely chop larger ones.

350 g / 12 oz young carrots
3 spring onions
$\frac{1}{2}$ organic uncoated orange
5 tbsp olive oil
1 tbsp sherry vinegar
2 or 3 sprigs of fresh coriander
2 tbsp pine nuts
salt and pepper

1   Rinse the carrots and grate them in the food processor, using the shredding blade. Tip into a salad bowl and snip over the spring onions.

2   Grate 1 teaspoon of zest from the orange and extract 1 tablespoon of juice.

3   Mix the oil and vinegar together with the orange zest and juice. Season to taste with salt and pepper and pour over the dressing.

4   Snip over the coriander, sprinkle over the pine nuts and toss well to coat all the ingredients with the dressing.

GRILLED RADICCHIO with GOATS' CHEESE

🕐 *under 10 minutes*

For this sort of treatment use one of the logs of factory-made goats' cheese which are more economical. Cut it in slices about 6 mm / $\frac{1}{4}$ in thick.

2 small heads of radicchio
4 thick slices of fresh goats' cheese
2 tbsp olive oil
6 basil leaves
2 or 3 sprigs of fresh thyme
salt and pepper

1   Preheat a hot grill.

2   Cut the radicchio heads lengthwise in halves and take out a few of the centre leaves to create a hollow. Arrange the radicchio, cut side up, on 4 flameproof dishes.

3   Put a slice of cheese in each cavity and brush the leaves and cheese with the oil.

4   Snip over the basil and thyme. Season with pepper and a little salt on the leaves only.

5   Grill until the cheese is bubbling.

WARM MUSHROOMS à LA GRECQUE

🕐 *under 10 minutes*

This treatment also works very well with drained canned artichoke hearts instead of mushrooms.

450 g / 1 lb mushrooms
1 tsp coriander seeds
1 garlic clove
3 tbsp olive oil
½ tsp ground cumin
2 tbsp white wine
2 or 3 sprigs of flat-leaf parsley
2 or 3 sprigs of fresh coriander

1 Wipe the mushrooms and halve or slice them if they are too large. Lightly crush the coriander seeds.

2 Rub a sauté pan with the garlic clove. Heat the oil in it over a moderate heat, add the cumin and coriander seeds. Sauté for 1 minute and then add the mushrooms. Sauté for another 3–4 minutes, stirring frequently.

3 Add the wine and cook for 1 or 2 minutes more over a high heat.

4 Season to taste with salt and pepper. Snip over the parsley and coriander leaves, mix well and serve.

STIR-FRIED EGGS with PRAWNS and MANGE-TOUT PEAS

🕐 *under 10 minutes*

The secret of this dish is light cooking. Do not overcook the eggs – they should be just set but still slightly moist.

115 g / 4 oz mange-tout peas
½ lemon
170 g / 6 oz peeled cooked prawns
1 tbsp oil
3 spring onions
½ tsp soy sauce
4 eggs
salt and pepper

1 Top and tail the mange-tout peas. Squeeze the juice from the lemon and toss the prawns in it.

2 In a frying pan or wok, heat the oil over a moderate to high heat and snip in the spring onions. Stir-fry for a minute or two and then snip in the mange-tout peas in 1 cm / ½ in chunks. Cook for 2 more minutes.

3 Drain the prawns and add them with the soy sauce. Stir-fry for about a minute.

4 Beat the eggs lightly with 2 tablespoons of water and some salt and pepper and pour these into the wok. Stir-fry until the eggs are just firm but still moist.

EGGS en COCOTTE with SPINACH

🕐 *under 15 minutes*

55 g / 2 oz butter
55 g / 2 oz fresh young leaf spinach
large pinch of grated nutmeg
4 tbsp single cream
4 eggs
1 tbsp grated Parmesan
salt and pepper

1 Heat the oven to 180C / 350F / gas4 and boil a kettle full of water.

2 Use half the butter to coat the sides and bases of 4 ramekins.

3 Into each ramekin snip some spinach and sprinkle some nutmeg. Then trickle in 1 tablespoon of cream and season with salt and pepper. Break an egg into each.

4 Dot the top of each ramekin with the remaining butter, sprinkle with the cheese and place them in a deep-sided baking dish.

5 Pour in the boiling water from the kettle, so that it comes at least halfway up the sides of the ramekins.

6 Bake in the oven for 7-10 minutes, depending on how well set you wish the eggs to be.

Variations:
1 There are innumerable variations on this classic dish: try replacing the spinach with watercress, chives, sorrel or mushrooms.

2 Instead of vegetables, use grated cheese, flaked smoked haddock or strips of smoked salmon as flavouring additions.

MINI CAULIFLOWERS in STILTON SAUCE

◕ *under 15 minutes*

If mini cauliflowers are not available, divide a fresh firm large one into 4, removing the woody core.

4 baby cauliflowers
55 g / 2 oz butter
55 g / 2 oz flour
250 ml / 8 fl oz milk
170 g / 6 oz Stilton
2 tbsp port
pinch of cayenne
salt and pepper

1   Heat some water in a kettle. Take off most of the outside leaves of the cauliflowers, trim their bases and cut a deep cross into them.

2   Put them in a large pan, sprinkle lightly with salt and cover them with the boiling water. Place over a high heat and bring to the boil, then cover and simmer gently for about 10 minutes until just tender.

3   Meanwhile, melt the butter in a saucepan over a moderate heat and add the flour. Stir with a wooden spoon to mix into a roux and cook for 2-3 minutes until smooth and just beginning to colour.

4   Gradually add the milk and then cook, stirring, for a few minutes until thick and smooth.

5   Off the heat, crumble in the cheese, add the port, and season to taste. Mix well until the cheese has all melted.

6   Drain the cooked cauliflowers well and place one on each of 4 plates. Pour the sauce over them and sprinkle very lightly with cayenne.

SMOKED EEL FILLETS with APPLE and MUSTARD SAUCE

◕ *under 10 minutes*

If the eel fillets are small allow 2 per person.

1 tbsp olive oil
2 spring onions
2 sharp firm apples
½ lemon
4 tbsp sour cream
2 tbsp grainy mustard
2 tbsp horseradish sauce
small bunch of dill or rocket
4 smoked eel fillets
salt and pepper

1   Put the oil in a sauté pan over a moderate heat. Snip in the spring onions and sauté for 1 or 2 minutes.

2   Meanwhile, halve the apples and core them. Then grate or chop them coarsely. Squeeze the juice from the lemon.

3   Add the apples to the pan with the cream, mustard, horseradish and 1 or 2 tablespoons of the lemon juice. Season to taste with salt and pepper. Snip in most of the herbs and cook gently for 1 or 2 minutes.

4   Pour the sauce on 4 plates and place a smoked eel fillet in the middle of each. Dribble a little more lemon juice over each fillet and snip over a little of the reserved herbs.

PAPAYA with SMOKED MACKEREL MOUSSE

◕ *under 10 minutes*

Use only perfectly ripe papayas and, if possible, try to chill them beforehand for better flavour and easier preparation.

350 g / 12 oz skinned smoked mackerel fillets
100 ml / 3½ fl oz crème fraîche or sour cream
4 tbsp horseradish sauce
1 tsp tomato paste
1 lemon
2 or 3 drops Tabasco
2 ripe papayas
salt and pepper

1   Flake the fish fillets into the food processor. Add the cream, horseradish, tomato paste and the juice of half the lemon. Whizz until smooth. Season to taste with the Tabasco and salt and pepper. Whizz again briefly to mix.

2   Peel and halve the papayas. Remove their seedy cores and halve each half again into quarters.

3   On each plate put a mound of the mousse and then place 2 quarters of papaya side by side, concave sides around the mousse to sandwich it closely so that there is a thick band of filling between them.

4   Sprinkle with the juice of the remaining lemon half to serve.

King Prawns Sautéed with Ginger and Chilli

KING PRAWNS SAUTÉED *with* GINGER *and* CHILLI

🕐 *under 10 minutes*

12 unpeeled cooked king prawns
piece of fresh ginger about 1 cm/½ in across
2 garlic cloves
1 small chilli pepper
1 lemon
2 tbsp sunflower oil
2 tsp sesame oil
salt and pepper

1 Rinse the unpeeled prawns and pat them dry. If preferred, twist off their heads and tails.

2 Peel the ginger. Cut the chilli in half and remove its seeds.

3 Whizz the garlic, ginger and chilli in the food processor. Add the juice from the lemon along with half the sunflower oil and whizz again briefly.

4 Heat the sesame oil and the remaining sunflower oil in a sauté pan or wok over a moderate heat.

5 Add the ginger and chilli mixture and stir-fry for about 2 or 3 minutes.

6 Add the prawns and stir-fry for another 2 minutes.

Variation:
To make these into canapés to serve with drinks, use shelled king prawns and fry 3 slices of bread in 1 tablespoon of sesame oil with a small knob of butter and 2 tablespoons of sesame seeds. Cut each slice into 4 triangles and serve each of the prawns on one, coated with the pan juices and sesame seeds.

TARTINIS

As baking is the one thing you cannot do in a matter of minutes, we have made a point of devising several snacks and starters using the wide range of flavoured breads, scones and muffins now so readily available. Our 'tartini' is a cross between the French tartine, *or open sandwich, and the Italian* crostini, *or toasted open sandwich.*

MOZZARELLA, ANCHOVY and CAPERS on TOAST

🕐 *under 15 minutes*

1 small can of flat anchovies in oil
8 slices of crusty white bread
2 tbsp capers
1 large mozzarella
pepper

1   Heat the grill. Drain the anchovies, reserving their oil, and halve or cut them into small lengths.

2   Toast the bread on one side.

3   Brush the untoasted side with the oil from the anchovies, arrange the anchovy fillets on top and sprinkle each with a few capers.

4   Slice the cheese fairly thinly and arrange over the bread. Sprinkle with pepper.

5   Grill until very hot and the cheese is bubbling.

Variation:
Onion bread is also good in this dish.

BABY TOMATO and PESTO MINI PIZZAS

🕐 *under 15 minutes*

Use 'passata', chopped tomato concentrate, rather than tomato paste. Or, if necessary, boil down some ordinary tinned chopped tomatoes.

4 ciabatta baps
100 g / $3\frac{1}{2}$ oz mozzarella
170 g / 6 oz cherry tomatoes
1 garlic clove
1 tbsp olive oil
4 tbsp tomato concentrate
100 ml / $3\frac{1}{2}$ fl oz pesto sauce
about 16 basil leaves
salt and pepper

1   Heat a hot grill.

2   Cut the baps across in halves and thinly slice the mozzarella. Halve the cherry tomatoes and crush the garlic.

3   In a bowl, mix the olive oil, tomato concentrate, garlic and pesto sauce. Season to taste with pepper.

4   Spread this mixture over the bap halves and cover with the mozzarella slices. Dot with the halved tomatoes.

5   Grill until the cheese is bubbling.

6   Snip over the basil leaves and sprinkle with more pepper to serve.

Variation:
Use a ready-made pizza base and cut with a pastry cutter to get the right size.

ASPARAGUS TIPS and ANCHOVY PASTE on MUFFINS

🕐 *under 10 minutes*

8 anchovy fillets
1 tbsp capers
6 tbsp olive oil
1 lemon
4 muffins
1 can (170 g / 6 oz) of asparagus tips
salt and pepper

1   Heat a hot grill. Drain and wipe the anchovies to take off some of the salt.

2   Snip them into the food processor with the capers, oil, the juice of half the lemon and some pepper. Whizz to a smooth paste.

3   Split the muffins in half, toast them lightly and spread them thickly with the paste. Drain the asparagus tips well and then arrange them on the muffin halves.

4   Sprinkle with a little more lemon juice and pepper. Heat through again briefly under the grill.

Variations:
1   Use fresh asparagus tips, steamed lightly for about 3 minutes or blanched for 2 minutes.

2   Hard-boil an egg while making this tartini, then shell it and grate it over the asparagus.

Top: Baby Tomato and Pesto Mini Pizzas; Bottom: Asparagus Tips and Anchovy Paste on Muffins

CREAM of MUSHROOM MUFFINS

🕐 *under 20 minutes*

This is even tastier with a few wild mushrooms.

115 g / 4 oz browncap mushrooms
55 g / 2 oz butter
4 muffins
4 tbsp white wine
150 ml / ¼ pt crème fraîche
pinch of freshly grated nutmeg
small bunch of chives
salt and pepper

1 Heat the grill until hot. Slice the mushrooms, or halve them if small.

2 Melt one-third of the butter in a sauté pan over a moderate to high heat and add the mushrooms with some seasoning. Sauté until they give off their liquid.

3 While the mushrooms are cooking, split the muffins and toast them lightly.

4 Remove the cooked mushrooms with a slotted spoon and keep warm. Add the wine to the sauté pan and reduce over a high heat until only 1 or 2 tablespoons of liquid are left.

5 Stir in the cream and reduce again until it has a good thick consistency. Beat in the remaining butter and then add a little nutmeg and adjust the seasoning, if necessary.

6 Spread a little of the cream sauce on the toasted muffin halves.

7 Return the mushrooms to the pan and mix well with the sauce.

8 Spoon the mushroom cream on the muffin halves, snip over the chives and serve.

GUACAMOLE on WALNUT BREAD

🕐 *under 10 minutes*

The guacamole also makes a very good dip. Serve it with tortilla chips.

2 small green chillis
4 spring onions
2 or 3 sprigs of coriander
2 firm ripe tomatoes
2 large ripe avocados
1 lime
4 slices of walnut bread
salt and pepper

1 Halve the chillis and remove their seeds. Snip them into the bowl of the food processor, followed by the spring onions and coriander.

2 Chop the tomatoes coarsely and peel, stone and coarsely chop the avocados.

3 Add both to the food processor with the juice of half the lime. Whizz until just smooth, but still with a bit of texture.

4 Season to taste with salt and pepper and add a little more lime juice, if necessary, but do not allow to become too liquid.

5 Cut the walnut bread slices in halves or quarters and spread the mixture thickly on them.

Variation:
If you can't get walnut bread, onion bread works equally well.

GRAVLAX and CRÈME FRAÎCHE on RYE BREAD

🕐 *under 10 minutes*

Packets of gravlax frequently come with their own pack of dill mustard sauce – but never enough! Try mixing this into the cream in place of the mustard and herbs.

100 ml / 3½ fl oz crème fraîche or sour cream
1 tbsp sweet mustard, preferably dill mustard
½ lemon
4 slices of rye bread
whites of 2 spring onions
115 g / 4 oz gravlax
small sprig of dill leaves
salt and pepper

1 In a bowl, mix the cream with the mustard and 1 or 2 tablespoons of lemon juice. Do not add too much lemon juice or the sauce will become too runny. Season to taste with salt and pepper.

2 Cut the slices of bread across diagonally into triangles and snip the spring onions over them. Spoon two-thirds of the cream mixture over them and then arrange the gravlax on top.

3 Spoon the remaining mixture in large dollops on top of the gravlax. Snip the dill over the tops.

BRUSCHETTA with CIABATTA

🌓 *under 10 minutes*

This is an excellent way of using up very ripe squashy tomatoes.

1 loaf of ciabatta bread
2 garlic cloves
2 tbsp olive oil
1 very ripe large tomato
55 g / 2 oz Parmesan
salt and pepper

1 Heat a hot grill.

2 Halve the loaf lengthwise horizontally and grill lightly on both sides. Leave the grill on.

3 Rub the cut surfaces with the garlic and then brush with the oil.

4 Halve the tomato. Smear one half over each slice of bread, leaving the pulp spread on the bread.

5 Season with pepper and grate over the Parmesan.

6 Return to the grill briefly until the cheese melts, then cut each piece of bread in half to serve.

Left to right: Gravlax and Crème Fraîche on Rye Bread, Potato Scones with Maple-cure Bacon and Blue Cheese (page 36) and Guacamole on Walnut Bread

POTATO SCONES with MAPLE-CURE BACON and BLUE CHEESE

🕐 *under 15 minutes*

If maple-cure bacon is unavailable, any sweet-cure unsmoked variety will do.

170 g / 6 oz Danish blue cheese
4 slices of maple-cure bacon
4 potato scones
pinch of cayenne
freshly ground black pepper

1 Heat a hot grill and cut the cheese in slices.

2 Grill the bacon until well cooked on both sides.

3 About halfway through the cooking, put the scones under the grill with the bacon and toast one side of them until lightly coloured.

4 Brush the untoasted side lightly with a little of the bacon fat from the grill pan.

5 Cut each slice of bacon in two and arrange them in pairs on each scone and then cover with blue cheese.

6 Season with pepper and grill until the cheese is bubbling.

7 Sprinkle lightly with cayenne and serve cut across in half.

HERBY SCRAMBLED EGGS on MUFFINS

🕐 *under 10 minutes*

55 g / 2 oz butter
8 eggs
2 tbsp single cream
few drops Worcestershire sauce
4 tbsp finely snipped mixed fresh herbs,
    preferably parsley, savory, thyme, chives or
    tarragon
4 muffins
salt and pepper

1 Melt two-thirds of the butter in a heavy-bottomed pan over a gentle heat.

2 Break the eggs into a small bowl and beat them lightly. Stir in the cream, Worcestershire sauce, most of the herbs and salt and pepper to taste.

3 Pour the mixture into the pan and cook, stirring continuously, until the eggs are just beginning to set.

4 While the eggs are cooking, split the muffins and toast them lightly. Spread the halves with a little of the remaining butter.

5 Spoon the eggs on the muffin halves, put a small pat of butter on each and sprinkle lightly with the reserved herbs.

STIR-FRIED SPRING ONION and PARMA HAM CROÛTES

🕐 *under 10 minutes*

The spring onion and Parma ham mixture also makes the basis of a good salad. Toss it with watercress or lambs' lettuce.

2 tbsp olive oil
2 garlic cloves
12 leafy spring onions
small sprig of lemon thyme
$\frac{1}{2}$ lemon
4 thin slices of Parma ham
4 thick slices of crusty white Italian bread
salt and pepper

1 Put the oil in a sauté pan over a low to moderate heat and crush the garlic into it. Cook for 1 or 2 minutes.

2 Turn up the heat to high and snip the spring onions into the pan in 5 cm / 2 in lengths, followed by the lemon thyme and the juice of the lemon. Season well with salt and pepper.

3 Put the ham slices on top of each other, roll them into a cylinder and then snip this in narrow strips over the pan.

4 Sauté for a few minutes until the spring onions are just tender but still slightly crunchy. Season.

5 Arrange the mixture on the slices of bread to serve.

PASTA

Pasta is a great standby for the quick cook. You can keep a wide variety of dried pasta in the store-cupboard and make your own sauce in a matter of minutes – some do not even require cooking and are simply stirred into the cooked and drained pasta. Always take the time to grate any accompanying Parmesan freshly. Ready-grated cheese has little of the taste or pungency of the original.

BASIC RECIPE for COOKING PASTA

◗ *under 15 minutes*

The exact cooking time of dried pasta will depend on the type and thickness of the pasta as well as its age. Do not go too much by times on packets: test as you cook; it should be just tender but still firm to the bite. Fresh pasta, of course, cooks in a matter of minutes. Speed up the process by heating half the water in a kettle.

450 g / 1 lb dried pasta
1 or 2 tbsp olive oil
2 tbsp salt

1 Put 4.5 l / 8 pt of water in a large pan and put on a high heat. Alternatively, to speed things up, heat half the water in the pan and the other half in the kettle. Add the salt and 1 tablespoon of oil to the water in the pan.

2 While the water is heating start making the sauce.

3 When the water is boiling rapidly, put in the pasta. If it is in long strands like spaghetti, break the strands cleanly in half, in handfuls, before adding it to the water. Bring back to a good rolling boil and cook rapidly until the pasta is tender but still firm to the bite.

4 Drain the cooked pasta well.

5 If using a no-cook sauce, return the drained pasta to the pan and stir the sauce into it over a gentle heat for a minute or so. Otherwise, stir the remaining oil into the drained pasta to keep the strands from sticking together, put it in a warmed serving dish and pour the sauce over it.

NO·COOK SAUCES

These sauces are very quickly prepared and are simply stirred into the pasta after it has been drained and returned to the pan over a gentle heat. This is sufficient to warm the sauce through or cook it slightly should that be necessary.

QUICK CARBONARA

🕐 *under 10 minutes*

2 eggs
150 ml/$\frac{1}{4}$ pt single cream
55 g/2 oz Parmesan
2 slices of Parma ham
1 thick slice of smoked ham
2 or 3 sprigs of flat-leaf parsley

1 In a large bowl, lightly beat the eggs and then mix in the cream.

2 Grate in the Parmesan and season to taste. Snip in the meats and parsley.

3 Put the cooked and drained pasta back in the pan. Add the sauce and toss well over a gentle heat to coat the pasta thoroughly with the mixture.

CRUSHED NUT VINAIGRETTE

🕐 *under 15 minutes*

This sauce, based on a classic Italian dish, goes especially well with thin noodles. such as spaghettini or vermicelli, and is best served without any accompanying cheese. You can vary the nuts according to preference and, if you have the time, toasting the almonds produces a memorable flavour.

4 tbsp shelled blanched almonds
4 tbsp shelled pistachios
2 garlic cloves
3 tbsp olive oil
1 tbsp walnut oil
1 tbsp lemon juice
4 tbsp pine nuts
2 or 3 sprigs of parsley
5 or 6 basil leaves
salt and pepper

1 Put the almonds and pistachios in the food processor with the garlic and whizz briefly until coarsely chopped. Do not over-process.

2 In a cup or small bowl, mix the olive oil and the walnut oil with the lemon juice and salt and pepper to taste.

3 Pour the vinaigrette over the cooked and drained pasta returned to the pan over a gentle heat and mix well to coat thoroughly.

4 Sprinkle in the crushed nut mixture, the whole pine nuts and snip over the herbs. Toss well again and serve.

SALAMI, PARSLEY and OLIVES

🕐 *under 10 minutes*

Use a good strong Italian or Lyons salami for this dish, or try some of the more exotic varieties, such as those made from wild boar or studded with pistachio nuts. A light pink salami looks very good against green pasta. Garlic-flavoured olives give the best result.

12 thick slices of salami
3 or 4 sprigs of flat-leaf parsley
115 g/4 oz stoned black olives
2 tbsp olive oil
pepper

1 Cut the slices of salami into strips. Into a bowl, snip these strips into cubes. Then snip in the parsley and olives.

2 Pour the oil over the cooked and drained pasta returned to the pan. Then scatter over the contents of the bowl and season generously with pepper. Mix in well over a gentle heat.

Spaghettini verdi with Salami, Parsley and Olives

TOMATO and FENNEL

🕐 *under 10 minutes*

½ head of fennel, with plenty of feathery tops
450 g / 1 lb ripe tomatoes
1 spring onion
1 garlic clove
2 tbsp olive oil
pinch of sugar (optional)
salt and pepper

1　Take off the outer stalks from the fennel, remove the woody core and reserve the feathery leaves.

2　Whizz the tomatoes, fennel, spring onion and garlic together in the food processor until coarsely chopped.

3　Mix in just enough olive oil to give the sauce a good thick consistency and season well. Add a little sugar, if necessary.

4　Mix the sauce into the cooked and drained pasta returned to the pan over a gentle heat. Snip over the reserved fennel leaves.

SMOKED SALMON, SOUR CREAM and CHIVES

🕐 *under 15 minutes*

This sauce goes best with thin noodles, such as spaghettini.

1 lemon
300 ml / ½ pt sour cream
1 spring onion
115 g / 4 oz smoked salmon
bunch of chives
pepper

1　In a bowl, mix the juice of half the lemon into the cream along with some pepper. Snip in the spring onion and mix well.

2　Into another bowl, snip the salmon into thin strips about 2 cm / ¾ in long.

3　Pour the cream mixture over the cooked and drained pasta returned to the pan and mix in well over a gentle heat.

4　Scatter over the salmon and snip in the chives.

5　Toss well and serve with the remaining half lemon cut in wedges.

COOKED SAUCES

Apart from the Quick Bolognese, all of these sauces may be made in about the time it takes to cook the pasta itself.

WILTED SPINACH LEAVES and BACON

🕐 *under 10 minutes*

2 thick slices of smoked bacon
1 garlic clove
225 g / 8 oz baby spinach leaves
2 tbsp oil
1 tsp soy sauce
pepper

1 Snip the bacon into a non-stick frying pan and dry-fry until crisp. Remove the bacon.

2 Crush the garlic, put it in the pan and sauté for 1 or 2 minutes, stirring frequently.

3 Snip handfuls of the spinach leaves into the pan in large shreds. Sauté over a fairly high heat until the spinach is just wilted, stirring frequently.

4 Reduce the heat and stir in the oil and soy sauce. Snip in the cooked bacon and season with pepper.

5 Stir into the cooked and drained pasta.

LEEK and CHEDDAR

🕐 *under 10 minutes*

A few halved baby leeks also work very well in this dish.

1 large leek
115 g / 4 oz Cheddar
2 tbsp olive oil
1 tsp Dijon mustard
$\frac{1}{2}$ lemon
2 tbsp single cream
pinch of nutmeg
3 or 4 sprigs of parsley

1 Halve the leek and rinse it well under running water to remove any grit. Pat it dry and shred it. Coarsely grate the cheese.

2 Heat the oil in a sauté pan over a moderate heat and sauté the shredded leek in it for a minute or two, until just softened.

3 Stir in the mustard, the juice of the half lemon, the cream and nutmeg and cook for another minute.

4 Stir the sauce into the drained and cooked pasta, sprinkle in the cheese and toss well, then snip over the parsley.

PRAWN, SUGAR PEAS and CHILLI OIL

🕐 *under 10 minutes*

This sauce is best suited to round noodles or thinner pasta. If sugar peas are unobtainable, mange-tout work equally well.

170 g / 6 oz sugar peas
1 garlic clove
3 tbsp chilli oil
1 tbsp sherry vinegar
170 g / 6 oz peeled cooked prawns
salt and pepper

1 Cut the peas into short lengths and crush the garlic.

2 Heat the oil in a sauté pan over a moderate heat. Add the garlic to the pan and sauté for 1 or 2 minutes, stirring frequently.

3 Add the peas and the vinegar. Sauté for 3 or 4 minutes, then add the prawns and sauté for 1 minute more.

4 Season to taste and stir into the cooked and drained pasta.

QUICK BOLOGNESE

◗ *under 30 minutes*

The better the quality of the minced steak, the better this sauce will be: ordinary mince is too fatty and will therefore not brown successfully.

2 tbsp oil
55 g / 2 oz streaky bacon
1 spring onion
1 stalk of celery
1 garlic clove
225 g / 8 oz minced steak
100 ml / $3\frac{1}{2}$ fl oz red wine
225 g / 8 oz can of chopped tomatoes
3 or 4 sprigs of flat-leaf parsley
$\frac{1}{2}$ tsp Worcestershire sauce
2 tsp tomato paste
$\frac{1}{2}$ tbsp dried oregano
salt and pepper

1 Heat the oil in a large sauté pan over a moderate heat. Snip in the bacon, spring onion and celery and crush in the garlic. Cook for 2 or 3 minutes, stirring frequently.

2 Turn up the heat to high, add the meat and mix well. Press the mixture down into a flat cake and cook until the meat on the underside is well browned and beginning to stick to the pan.

3 Break up the cake, turning the meat, and then re-form it and repeat the process. Do this once more, or until the meat is uniformly browned.

4 Add the wine, mix well and boil until the wine is mostly cooked off.

5 Add the tomatoes with their liquid and snip in the parsley. Add the Worcestershire sauce, tomato paste and oregano. Season and mix well. Bring to the boil and simmer rapidly for 10 minutes.

POACHED BABY VEGETABLES

◗ *under 10 minutes*

Use a wide variety of tiny baby vegetables in this sauce, as long as they are fresh and tender. Cherry tomatoes and florets of young broccoli also work well.

225 g / 8 oz tiny baby carrots
225 g / 8 oz baby sweetcorn
225 g / 8 oz baby French beans
225 g / 8 oz baby courgettes
150 ml / $\frac{1}{4}$ pt olive oil
2 tbsp balsamic vinegar
4 or 5 sprigs of flat-leaf parsley
salt and pepper

1 Put 5 mm / $\frac{1}{4}$ in of water in a wide saucepan and add a large pinch of salt. Put in all the vegetables, in a single layer if possible, cover the pan tightly and bring to the boil.

2 Simmer for 3 or 4 minutes, until the vegetables are just tender, but still crunchy.

3 While the vegetables are cooking, mix the oil and vinegar and snip in the parsley. Season to taste.

4 Drain the vegetables, put them into a warmed bowl and pour the vinaigrette over them. Mix well and then stir into the cooked and drained pasta.

CHICKEN LIVERS and CELERY

◗ *under 10 minutes*

225 g / 8 oz chicken livers
2 stalks of celery
2 tbsp oil
1 spring onion
1 garlic clove
2 or 3 sprigs of parsley
2 tbsp port or Madeira
6 tbsp double cream
cayenne
salt and pepper

1 Trim and slice the chicken livers. Rinse them and pat dry. Trim off any coarse fibres from the celery stalks and chop them into fine strips.

2 Heat the oil in a sauté pan over a moderate heat

3 Snip in the spring onion. Crush the garlic and add it. Snip over most of the parsley and add the celery. Sauté for a minute or two.

4 Add the chicken livers and sauté for a few minutes, depending on how pink you wish the livers to be.

5 Add the wine and sauté for a minute or so more to reduce it.

6 Stir in the cream, season to taste with cayenne, salt and pepper and heat gently to warm through.

7 Stir into the cooked and drained pasta and snip over the remaining parsley.

TUNA FISH, RED ONION and OLIVE OIL

🕐 *under 10 minutes*

The red onion is essential for this dish; ordinary onions will not give the same result. If you do not have any lemon mayonnaise, finely grate some lemon zest into ordinary mayonnaise.

1 red onion
2 tbsp olive oil
1 can (200 g / 7 oz) tuna fish in oil
$\frac{1}{2}$ lemon
1 tbsp capers
2 tbsp lemon mayonnaise
salt and pepper

1 Slice the onion into thin rings.

2 Heat the oil in a sauté pan over a moderate heat and cook the onion in it for a minute or two.

3 Drain the tuna fish and flake the flesh into the pan. Add the juice from the lemon, along with the capers, mayonnaise and salt and pepper to taste.

4 Cook for another 2 or 3 minutes, stirring frequently, to warm the fish through and then pour over the cooked and drained pasta.

Conchiglie with Tuna Fish, Red Onion and Olive Oil

4

MAIN COURSES

Our main courses are mostly hot and based on fish, meat and poultry, although there are also some main course salads in the next chapter. To cook at speed it is generally wisest to spend that little bit extra on prime quality cuts which are the most tender and best suit quick cooking. Also, ready-prepared fish and meats, although again more expensive, cut down drastically on preparation times.

For many of our main courses the greater part of the work is in the initial stages so that the dish can be left to finish, often covered with a lid, while the first course is being enjoyed.

Lamb Chops with Apricot, Cumin and Garlic Sauce (page 62) accompanied by Baby New Potatoes (page 72) with Orange and Lemon Butter (page 51)

STRIPS

Tender cuts of meat and poultry and firm-fleshed fish cook very quickly when sliced into thin strips. Start by cutting the meat into slices about 5mm/ $\frac{1}{4}$ in thick and then cut these across into pieces about 5–7.5 cm/ 2–3 in long and 2.5 cm/ 1 in wide. Try to cut with the grain as this helps make the strips more tender, gives a better texture and reduces shrinkage during cooking. Strips are best cooked by either sautéing them or stir-frying them in a wok. Make sure the pan is hot enough when they go in to seal the meat quickly so that it keeps its juices.

VEAL STRIPS with MUSTARD CREAM SAUCE

🕐   *under 10 minutes*

450 g/1 lb veal escalopes
30 g/1 oz butter
1 tbsp oil
1 spring onion
1 garlic clove
1 tsp white wine vinegar
6 tbsp single cream
1 tbsp grainy mustard
1 tsp sweet mustard
pinch of paprika
salt and pepper

1   Cut the veal escalopes into strips.

2   Melt the butter with the oil in a wok over a moderate to high heat. Snip in the spring onion and crush in the garlic. Stir-fry for 1 or 2 minutes.

3   Add the veal strips and stir-fry for 2 or 3 minutes.

4   Add the vinegar and stir-fry for a minute or two until it is almost all driven off.

5   Reduce the heat. Stir in the cream and mustards. Cook gently until warmed through, season to taste and sprinkle with paprika to serve.

BEEF STRIPS with TOMATOES and HORSERADISH

🕐   *under 10 minutes*

Horseradish sauces and creams come in widely differing degrees of potency, so add them with caution.

450 g/1 lb fillet steak
225 g/8 oz ripe tomatoes
4 shallots
1 tbsp red wine vinegar
2 tbsp creamed horseradish
55 g/2 oz butter
2 tbsp oil
salt and pepper

1   Cut the beef into strips. Coarsely chop the tomatoes and shallots. Whizz them in the food processor until smooth. Add the vinegar and horseradish and season to taste.

2   Melt half the butter with half the oil in a wok over a moderate to high heat and cook the sauce, stirring, for 2 or 3 minutes. Tip out into a warmed bowl and keep hot.

3   Add the remaining butter and oil to the wok and stir-fry the beef strips until well browned.

4   Lower the heat and return the sauce to the wok. Simmer gently for a minute or two. Adjust the seasoning, if necessary.

PORK STRIPS with PIZZAIOLA SAUCE

🕐 *under 15 minutes*

The pizzaiola sauce works equally well with beef and poultry.

450 g / 1 lb pork tenderloin
1 tbsp oil
salt and pepper
for the pizzaiola sauce:
2 green peppers
400 g / 14 oz ripe tomatoes
3 spring onions
2 garlic cloves
55 g / 2 oz flat mushrooms
2 tsp oregano
3 or 4 drops of Tabasco

1 Cut the pork into strips. Halve and deseed the green peppers. Coarsely chop the tomatoes.

2 Heat the oil in the wok over a high heat. Add the pork strips and peppers and stir-fry for 3 or 4 minutes.

3 Reduce the heat slightly. Snip in the spring onions and crush in the garlic. Stir-fry for 1 or 2 minutes.

4 Snip the mushrooms into the pan in thin strips and cook for 1 or 2 minutes more.

5 Add the tomatoes and oregano and bring to a simmer. Add the Tabasco and season to taste with salt and pepper. Cover and cook gently for about 5 minutes.

SALMON STRIPS with CUCUMBER and CRÈME FRAÎCHE

🕐 *under 10 minutes*

This dish is better if the cucumber is left unpeeled.

450 g / 1 lb salmon escalopes
½ cucumber
30 g / 1 oz butter
1 tbsp sunflower oil
3 tbsp white wine
6 tbsp crème fraîche
2 tbsp green peppercorns
small bunch of chives
salt and pepper

1 Cut the salmon into strips and chop the unpeeled cucumber into large matchstick strips.

2 Melt the butter with the oil in a wok over a moderate to high heat. Toss in the cucumber and stir-fry briefly. Add the salmon strips and stir-fry for 2 or 3 minutes.

3 Add the wine and keep stir-frying for a minute or two until it is almost all cooked off.

4 Reduce the heat and stir in the cream and green peppercorns. Season to taste, cook gently to heat through and snip over the chives to serve.

CHICKEN BREAST STRIPS *with* BLOOD ORANGE *and* WALNUTS

under 15 minutes

If blood orange juice is not available, try red grapefruit juice or an orange and red fruit juice mixture.

450 g / 1 lb boned and skinned chicken breasts
1 stalk of celery
55 g / 2 oz walnuts
30 g / 1 oz butter
1 tbsp oil
1 spring onion
2 garlic cloves
1 tbsp red wine vinegar
150 ml / $\frac{1}{4}$ pt blood orange juice
salt and pepper

1   Cut the chicken breasts into strips. Trim the celery and coarsely chop the walnuts.

2   Melt the butter with the oil in a wok over a moderate to high heat. Snip in the spring onion and celery. Crush in the garlic. Stir-fry for 1 or 2 minutes.

3   Increase the heat to high and add the chicken strips. Stir-fry for 3 or 4 minutes

4   Add the vinegar and stir-fry for a minute or so, until it is almost all driven off.

5   Stir in the orange juice with the chopped walnuts. Lower the heat and season to taste. Simmer gently for 5 minutes.

DUCK BREAST STRIPS *with* SWEETCORN *and* HONEY

🕐 *under 20 minutes*

If you wish, you can trim the fat off before cutting the duck into strips.

450 g / 1 lb duck breasts
1 tbsp honey
2 tsp light soy sauce
small pinch of five-spice powder
1 tbsp sherry vinegar
1 tbsp oil
6 baby sweetcorn
salt and pepper

1 Cut the duck into strips.

2 In a bowl, mix the honey, soy sauce, five-spice powder and half the vinegar. Stir in the duck strips so that they are well coated and leave to marinate for at least 5 minutes.

3 Drain the duck, reserving the marinade. Heat the oil in the wok over a high heat, tip in the drained duck strips and stir-fry for 2 or 3 minutes.

4 Lower the heat to moderate. Add the marinade and snip in the sweetcorn. Stir-fry for a minute or two more.

5 Pour into a warmed serving dish. Deglaze the pan with the remaining vinegar, adjust the seasoning and pour this over the duck.

Chicken Breast Strips with Blood Orange and Walnuts served on a bed of mixed salad leaves (see page 78)

FISH

Buy fish which has been pre-prepared as much as possible: whole fish should be gutted and, if necessary, scaled; fillets should be skinned and steaks should be cut quite thinly. It is essential not to over-cook fish: grilling should be brief at moderate temperatures and poaching at a very gentle simmer.

COD with TOMATO and WATERCRESS VINAIGRETTE

🕐 *under 10 minutes*

Most poached or grilled firm white fish suit this treatment.

1 spring onion
½ bay leaf
small sprig of dried thyme
2 tbsp white wine
4 or 5 sprigs of parsley
4 cod steaks or skinned fillets, each weighing about 140 g/5 oz
2 large ripe tomatoes
4 or 5 sprigs of watercress
1 tbsp white wine vinegar
2 tsp mustard
5 tbsp olive oil
salt and pepper

1 Heat some water in a kettle. Snip the spring onion into a large pan. Crumble in the bay leaf and the thyme. Add the white wine and snip in the stalks from the parsley. Add just enough boiling water to be able to cover the cod and season well.

2 Bring back to the boil and simmer gently for a minute or two. Add the cod and poach gently for about 5 minutes.

3 While the cod is poaching, make the vinaigrette: coarsely chop the tomatoes and whizz them in the food processor with most of the watercress, the vinegar and mustard.

4 With the machine still running, dribble in the oil. Season to taste and whizz briefly to mix.

5 Drain the cod well and pour over the vinaigrette. Garnish with the reserved watercress.

TWO-CHEESE COD

🕐 *under 15 minutes*

85 g/3 oz sharp mature Cheddar
55 g/2 oz Parmesan
1 tbsp olive oil
1 tbsp lemon juice
½ tsp mustard powder
pinch of nutmeg
4 cod steaks or skinned fillets, each weighing about 140 g/5 oz
pinch of cayenne
salt and pepper

1 Heat the grill. Slice the Cheddar thinly and grate the Parmesan.

2 Mix the oil with the lemon juice, mustard and nutmeg. Season well and brush the cod with the mixture.

3 Put the cod under the grill for a minute or two, turn carefully and brush the tops again with the dressing. Grill this side for a minute or so.

4 Cover the cod with slices of Cheddar and sprinkle generously with Parmesan. Season once more with pepper and grill again until the cheeses are bubbling and slightly browned.

5 Sprinkle lightly with cayenne and pepper to serve.

Variation:
A number of cheeses will work in place of the Cheddar: try a good strong Red Leicester or a blue cheese.

LEMON SOLE with ORANGE and LEMON BUTTER

under 10 minutes

4 large skinned lemon sole fillets
55 g / 2 oz butter
$\frac{1}{2}$ organic uncoated orange
$\frac{1}{2}$ organic uncoated lemon
salt and pepper

1 Heat the grill.

2 Season the fish with salt and pepper. Dice the butter. Peel off a few thin strips of zest from the orange and the lemon. Cut the fruit halves in half again and reserve one piece of each to serve. Squeeze the juice from the others and mix.

3 Whizz the pared zest in the food processor until finely chopped, add two-thirds of the butter and half the juice and season to taste. Whizz again briefly until well blended.

4 Brush some of the mixture over the tops of the fish fillets and grill for 2 or 3 minutes. Turn the fish carefully, spread some more of the flavoured butter over the fish and grill again for a minute or two more.

5 Deglaze the grill pan with the remaining juice and butter.

6 Season this sauce if necessary, pour it over the fish and serve with the remaining lemon and orange quarters cut into wedges.

Lemon Sole with Orange and Lemon Butter

SALMON ESCALOPES with MUSHROOM and PARSLEY CRUST

under 15 minutes

This dish works very well accompanied by the creamed mushrooms as served on muffins on page 34.

55 g / 2 oz mushrooms
2 tbsp oil
1 tbsp lemon juice
1 tbsp grainy mustard
2 tbsp dried breadcrumbs
1 spring onion
3 or 4 sprigs of parsley
4 salmon escalopes, each weighing about
   140 g / 5 oz
salt and pepper

1 Heat the grill until it is very hot. Finely chop the mushrooms.

2 In a bowl, mix the oil, lemon juice, mustard, mushrooms and breadcrumbs. Snip in the spring onion and most of the parsley, season generously and mix in well.

3 Grill the escalopes, skin side up, for 1 or 2 minutes. Turn them over, spread the mixture over the fleshy side of the escalopes and pat it into the flesh. Grill until the crust is firm and the fish is cooked to taste.

4 Leave to rest for about 1 minute and then snip over the remaining parsley to serve.

Salmon Strips with Cucumber and Crème Fraîche (page 47)

SALMON STEAKS with a LIGHT SALSA

under 15 minutes

If you don't have any chillis, just add some cayenne or Tabasco to taste.

1 small chilli pepper
100 g / 3½ oz ripe tomatoes
½ lime
2 tbsp olive oil
4 salmon steaks
3 spring onions
2 garlic cloves
3 or 4 sprigs of coriander
pinch of sugar
salt and pepper

1 Heat a hot grill. Halve the chilli and remove its seeds. Chop the tomatoes into fairly small pieces, squeeze the juice of the lime and crush the garlic.

2 In a bowl, mix half the lime juice with half the oil. Season with pepper and brush this mixture over both sides of the salmon steaks.

3 Grill the steaks for a few minutes on each side, until cooked to taste.

4 Meanwhile, heat the remaining oil in a sauté pan over a moderate heat. Snip in the spring onions and chilli and add the garlic. Cook for 2 or 3 minutes, stirring frequently.

5 Stir in the tomatoes, almost all the coriander and the remaining lime juice. Season to taste with salt, pepper and sugar. Cook for 2 or 3 minutes until the tomatoes are just softened.

6 Spoon a little of the salsa on each of 4 warmed plates, place a salmon steak on each and snip over the remaining coriander.

PAN-FRIED TROUT with NUT SAUCE

under 20 minutes

4 small gutted rainbow trout
2 garlic cloves
2 tbsp flour
55 g / 2 oz butter
2 tbsp oil
3 tbsp white wine
1 lemon
85 g / 3 oz slivered almonds
2 or 3 small sprigs of parsley
salt and pepper

1 Season the fish well inside and out. Crush the garlic cloves and divide one of them between the insides of each fish. Sprinkle the fish lightly with flour.

2 Melt half the butter with half the oil in a large frying pan over a high heat and brown the trout on both sides.

3 Turn the heat down and add the white wine and the juice from the lemon. Cover and leave to simmer for about 10 minutes, turning once.

4 While the fish are cooking, in a separate pan melt the remaining butter with the remaining oil over a moderate heat. Add the remaining garlic and cook for a minute or two. Add the nuts and sauté them, stirring frequently, until they are well browned.

5 When the fish are cooked, transfer them to warmed plates. Boil the liquid in the pan until only about 1 tablespoon is left. Then add the nut and garlic mixture to the pan and mix well.

6 Season the nut sauce, if necessary, pour it over the fish and snip over some parsley to serve.

POULTRY

Use corn-fed or free-range chicken for a better flavour. Thighs and drumsticks take longer to cook but have more taste than breast meat, so it is a good idea to use them in combination whenever possible. Chicken breasts are best cooked in a moist sauce to keep them from drying out.

QUICK POULE au POT with SMOKED HAM

🕐   *under 20 minutes*

2 boned and skinned chicken thighs
2 boned and skinned chicken breasts
1 onion
2 garlic cloves
2 stalks of celery
2 bay leaves
pinch of dried thyme
6 whole black peppercorns
2 or 3 sprigs of flat-leaf parsley
115 g/4 oz baby carrots
115 g/4 oz baby turnips
4 baby leeks
2 thick slices of cooked ham
2 tbsp capers
3 gherkins
150 ml/$\frac{1}{4}$ pt mayonnaise
salt and pepper

1   Heat some water in a kettle. Cut the chicken thighs and breasts in half lengthwise. Halve the onion and garlic cloves. Coarsely chop the celery.

2   Put enough of the hot water to cover the chicken in a large pan with the onion, crumbled bay leaves, celery, garlic, thyme, peppercorns, salt and the stalks from the parsley. Bring to the boil and simmer gently for a minute or two.

3   Add the chicken pieces and surround them with the carrots, turnips and leeks. Arrange the slices of ham over the top of the chicken pieces.

4   Bring back to the boil. Cover and simmer gently for about 10 minutes.

5   While the chicken is cooking, briefly whizz the parsley, capers and gherkins together in the food processor until coarsely chopped. Do not over-process. Add the mayonnaise and pepper to taste and whizz very briefly to mix well.

6   At the end of cooking time, take out the ham and leave to one side to cool slightly.

7   Transfer the chicken pieces and vegetables to a warmed serving dish with 3 or 4 tablespoons of the cooking liquid.

8   Dice the ham, discarding any fatty bits, and stir into the sauce with another 2 tablespoons of the cooking liquid. Serve this separately in a bowl.

GRILLED CHICKEN with DEVILLED RED FRUIT SAUCE

🕐   *under 20 minutes*

Speed the cooking by cutting the chicken thighs in half lengthwise.

8 small boned chicken thighs
2 tbsp oil
170 g/6 oz mixed red fruit conserves
$\frac{1}{2}$ tsp Worcestershire sauce
pinch of ground ginger
1 tbsp Dijon mustard
3 or 4 drops of Tabasco
3 tbsp crème fraîche or double cream
salt and pepper

1   Season the chicken thighs with salt and pepper.

2   Heat the oil in a large frying pan over a moderate to high heat. Cook the chicken thighs for 2–3 minutes on each side, until well browned.

3   Reduce the heat and add all the remaining ingredients, except the cream. Mix well, cover and simmer for about 10 minutes, turning the chicken halfway through.

4   Transfer the chicken to warmed plates and adjust the seasoning of the sauce.

5   Lightly fold the cream into the sauce so that it is streaked red and white. Heat through briefly and then spoon around the chicken.

CHICKEN DRUMSTICKS with SALSA VERDE

🕐 *under 20 minutes*

4 anchovy fillets in oil
½ lemon
4 or 5 sprigs of flat-leaf parsley
2 garlic cloves
1½ tbsp capers
1 tbsp soft brown sugar
4 tbsp oil
pinch of cayenne
8 small chicken drumsticks
salt and pepper

1 Heat the grill until very hot. Drain, pat dry and coarsely chop the anchovy fillets. Grate the zest from the lemon and squeeze its juice.

2 Put the anchovies in the food processor with the lemon zest, parsley, garlic, capers, sugar, 1 tablespoon of the oil, the cayenne and salt and pepper. Whizz until smooth.

3 Spread the chicken drumsticks with a little of the mixture and grill for about 10–15 minutes, turning 3 or 4 times to ensure even cooking.

4 When the drumsticks are nearly cooked, heat the remaining oil in a sauté pan over a moderate heat and cook the remaining sauce mixture for 2 or 3 minutes, stirring frequently.

5 Add the lemon juice, the remaining oil and adjust the seasoning if necessary.

6 Pour any juices from the grill pan into the sauce before serving.

CHICKEN in GOATS' CHEESE and CHIVE SAUCE

🕐 *under 15 minutes*

Use a piece of factory-made goats' cheese in log form. Cut off the rind before adding it to the sauce.

4 boned and skinned chicken breasts
2 tbsp oil
1 tbsp mustard
30 g/1 oz butter
85 g/3 oz soft goats' cheese
100 ml/3½ fl oz crème fraîche, double cream or
   fromage frais
pinch of celery salt
pinch of cayenne
bunch of chives
salt and pepper

1 Cut the chicken breasts in half lengthwise. Mix half the oil with the mustard and some pepper and brush this mixture over the chicken.

2 In a large sauté pan, melt the butter with the remaining oil over a moderate to high heat. Brown the chicken pieces for 2 or 3 minutes on each side and remove them from the pan.

3 Crumble in the goats' cheese and beat until completely melted. Stir in the cream. Season to taste with celery salt, pepper and cayenne.

4 Return the chicken to the pan and simmer gently for about 5 minutes.

5 Snip over the chives to serve.

STIR-FRIED CHICKEN, OYSTER MUSHROOMS and SPRING ONIONS

🕐 *under 15 minutes*

4 boned and skinned chicken breasts
1 tsp soy sauce
1 lemon
1 tsp sesame oil
1 tbsp sunflower oil
4 spring onions
1 garlic clove
85 g/3 oz oyster mushrooms
salt and pepper

1 Cut the chicken in large dice and toss in a bowl with the soy sauce, the juice from half the lemon and some pepper.

2 Heat the oils in a wok over a moderate to high heat. Snip in the spring onions, crush the garlic and add it. Stir-fry for 1 or 2 minutes.

3 Drain the chicken, reserving the liquid. Stir-fry the chicken pieces for 2 or 3 minutes.

4 Add the reserved liquid and stir-fry for a minute or so more until most of the liquid has been driven off.

5 Tear or snip in the mushrooms and stir-fry for 2 or 3 minutes more.

6 Adjust the seasoning, if necessary, sprinkle over the remaining lemon juice and stir-fry briefly to serve.

Variation:
Dribble the sesame oil over the dish as a dressing at the end instead of using it in the cooking.

CHICKEN in SWEET WHITE WINE

🕐 *under 20 minutes*

2 boned and skinned chicken breasts
2 boned and skinned chicken thighs
2 tbsp flour
pinch of celery salt
small pinch of dried sage
2 garlic cloves
30 g / 1 oz butter
1 tbsp oil
2 spring onions
150 ml / $\frac{1}{4}$ pt sweet white wine
2 tbsp crème fraîche or double cream
salt and pepper

1 Cut the chicken breasts and thighs in half lengthwise. Season the flour with celery salt, sage and pepper and dust the chicken pieces with it. Crush the garlic.

2 Melt the butter with the oil in a large frying pan over a moderate heat, snip in the spring onion and add the crushed garlic. Sauté for 2 or 3 minutes, stirring frequently.

3 Add the chicken pieces and pour in the wine. Cover and cook for about 8–10 minutes, turning the chicken pieces over halfway through.

4 Transfer the chicken to warmed plates. Boil the liquid in the pan to reduce it a little if necessary.

5 Stir in the cream, season to taste and pour over the chicken to serve.

Variation:
Add a few seedless grapes or raisins to the sauce with the cream.

CHICKEN BREASTS in COCONUT MILK with MANGO

🕐 *under 25 minutes*

4 boned and skinned chicken breasts
1 lime
1 not-too-ripe mango
100 ml / $3\frac{1}{2}$ fl oz thick coconut milk
1 tbsp sunflower oil
2 spring onions
pinch of ground ginger or cayenne
salt and pepper

1 Cut each breast in half lengthwise and season with the juice from the lime and pepper. Peel and slice the mango flesh, reserving all the juice.

2 Mix 1 tablespoon of the coconut milk with the sunflower oil and heat this in a large frying pan over a moderate heat. Snip in the spring onions and sauté them for 1 or 2 minutes, stirring frequently.

3 Add the chicken pieces and cook them for about 2 minutes on each side.

4 Add the remaining coconut milk and lime juice with the mango slices and juices. Cover the pan and simmer gently for 8 minutes, turning the chicken halfway through.

5 Transfer the chicken and mango pieces to warmed plates. Boil the sauce a little to reduce it slightly. Adjust the seasoning with salt and pepper if necessary, pour over the chicken and serve with a little ginger or cayenne sprinkled over the top.

Variation:
Crush in some pink peppercorns before boiling the sauce for even more colour and flavour.

DUCK BREASTS with BLACKCURRANT CONSERVE

🕐 *under 15 minutes*

If using the large French 'magrets', use only 2 and cut them in half lengthwise.

4 duck breasts
170 g / 6 oz blackcurrant conserve
4 tbsp red wine
1 tbsp green peppercorns
bunch of watercress
salt and pepper

1 Heat the grill until very hot.

2 Cut several deep diagonal incisions through the fat and into the flesh along the length of each breast. Season them with pepper.

3 Grill the duck for 5 minutes with the fat side uppermost, until the fat is crisp and deep golden. Turn them over and grill for another 5 minutes.

4 Meanwhile in a small pan, heat the blackcurrant conserve with the wine and green peppercorns. Season to taste and simmer gently until the duck is ready.

5 Put the duck on warmed plates and surround with sprigs of watercress.

6 Stir any juices from the grill pan into the sauce before serving separately.

Chicken Breasts in Coconut Milk with Mango

● *BEEF and VEAL*

The best and most tender fillet or sirloin steaks are expensive, but cook very rapidly and there is no waste as they are well trimmed.

BASIC GRILLED STEAK

🕐   *under 10 minutes*

Try to ensure that the steaks are at room temperature before cooking. If they come straight from the refrigerator they will shrink under the heat and will not cook satisfactorily in the short time involved. The grill must be very hot and the steaks should be as near the heat as possible so that the outsides seal quickly to keep in the juices. Turn the steaks with tongs or a spatula to avoid piercing them.

4 fillet or sirloin steaks, each weighing about
    140 g/5 oz and about 2 cm/$\frac{3}{4}$ in thick
1 tbsp oil
pepper

1   Heat the grill until it is very hot.

2   Brush the steaks on both sides with the oil and then season generously with pepper only.

3   Grill for 2 to 5 minutes on each side, depending on how well done you wish the steaks to be.

4   Serve topped with a pat of one of the savoury butters which follow.

● *SAVOURY BUTTERS*

These are easier to make if the butter is slightly soft. Use unsalted butter as it is then easier to adjust the seasoning. Put the butter mixtures on small squares of foil, roll them into a cylinder and freeze while the steaks are cooking. This may then be easily diced or sliced across into neat discs to place on the cooked steak.

If your food processor only has a large bowl, double the quantities and freeze the extra.

OLIVE and ANCHOVY BUTTER

🕐   *under 5 minutes*

55 g/2 oz butter
wedge of organic uncoated lemon
4 anchovy fillets in oil
55 g/2 oz stoned black olives
pepper

1   Dice the butter and coarsely chop the lemon wedge.

2   Drain, rinse and pat dry the anchovies. Snip them into the food processor and whizz with the lemon and olives until smooth.

3   Add the butter with pepper to taste and whizz again briefly until well mixed.

GARLIC and PARSLEY BUTTER

🕐 *under 5 minutes*

55 g / 2 oz butter
2 garlic cloves
2 or 3 sprigs of flat-leaf parsley
salt and pepper

1 Dice the butter.

2 In a food processor, whizz the butter with the garlic, parsley and seasoning to taste until smooth.

MUSTARD BUTTER

🕐 *under 5 minutes*

55 g / 2 oz butter
1 tbsp grainy mustard
1 tbsp Dijon mustard
1 tbsp lemon juice
pepper

1 Dice the butter.

2 In a food processor, whizz the butter with the mustards, lemon juice and pepper to taste until smooth.

BLUE CHEESE BUTTER

🕐 *under 5 minutes*

55 g / 2 oz butter
85 g / 3 oz blue cheese
1 tbsp port
6 whole black peppercorns

1 Dice the butter.

2 In a food processor, whizz the cheese with the port and peppercorns until fairly smooth.

3 Add the butter and whizz again briefly until well mixed.

VEAL ESCALOPES with LEMON and SAGE BUTTER

🕐 *under 10 minutes*

To dust small items with flour quickly use a small sieve or wire tea strainer.

2 tbsp flour
4 thinly beaten veal escalopes, each weighing
   about 85 g / 3 oz
1 lemon
55 g / 2 oz butter
1 tbsp oil
2 or 3 fresh sage leaves
salt and pepper

1   Season the flour with salt and pepper. Dust the escalopes lightly with the flour. Squeeze the juice from the lemon.

2   Melt the butter with the oil in a large frying pan over a moderate heat. Snip in the sage leaves and cook for 1 or 2 minutes.

3   Add the veal and cook for 2 minutes on each side.

4   Add half the lemon juice and seasoning to taste. Cook for 1 more minute over a very high heat, turning the veal halfway through.

5   Put the veal escalopes on warmed plates and deglaze the pan with the remaining lemon juice. Adjust the seasoning if necessary and pour over the veal to serve.

Calves' Liver with Lime

BEEF with MUSHROOM SAUCE

🕐 *under 15 minutes*

A more economical version of this dish may be made using minute steak.

12 black peppercorns
4 pieces of sirloin steak
225 g / 8 oz mushrooms
1 garlic clove
55 g / 2 oz butter
2 tbsp oil
2 spring onions
1 tbsp cognac
150 ml / $\frac{1}{4}$ pt single cream
salt and pepper
small bunch of chives

1   In the food processor coarsely crush the whole peppercorns and press them into the steaks. Slice the mushrooms thinly and crush the garlic.

2   Melt the butter with the oil in a large sauté pan over a moderate heat. Snip in the spring onions and add the garlic. Sauté for a minute or two, stirring frequently.

3   Increase the heat to high and sear the steaks for a minute or two on each side. Remove the steaks and keep them warm.

4   Reduce the heat again to moderate and add the mushrooms and cognac. Sauté for 2 or 3 minutes.

5   Stir in the cream, adjust the seasoning if necessary and return the steaks to the pan, along with any juices. Simmer gently for a few minutes, depending on how well done you wish the steaks to be.

6   Snip the chives over to serve.

CALVES' LIVER with LIME

🕐 *under 10 minutes*

The liver should be sliced paper-thin for best results. You may have to fry the slices one or two at a time. Liver is at its best if only cooked very briefly and still moist and pink inside. Increase the cooking times if you prefer liver well done, but be very careful as it quickly becomes tough if over-cooked.

1 uncoated lime
30 g / 1 oz butter
1 tbsp oil
3 spring onions
1 tbsp sherry vinegar
2 tbsp sweet vermouth
450 g / 1 lb very thin slices of calves' liver
salt and pepper

1   Zest the lime and squeeze its juice.

2   Melt the butter with the oil in a wok over a moderate to high heat. Snip in the spring onions and add the lime zest. Stir-fry for 1 or 2 minutes.

3   Add the sherry vinegar and vermouth with seasoning to taste and stir-fry until only about 1 tablespoon of liquid is left.

4   Turn up the heat to high and add the liver. Fry for 1 or 2 minutes only on each side. Tip out into a warmed serving dish.

5   Deglaze the pan with the lime juice, adjust the seasoning and pour this over the liver to serve.

LAMB

The better cuts of good quality lamb, including the small tender chops cut from the best end of neck and thin noisettes, cook quite quickly. The cooking times given are for slightly pink lamb. Add a few minutes more if you prefer your lamb well done. Make sure that the pieces of lamb are well trimmed of fat.

LAMB CHOPS with APRICOT, CUMIN and GARLIC SAUCE

● *under 25 minutes*

4 dried apricots
100 ml / 3½ fl oz white wine
8 small lamb chops
½ tsp ground cumin
½ organic uncoated lemon
2 garlic cloves
1 tbsp oil
2 spring onions
1 tbsp clear honey
salt and pepper

1   Coarsely chop the apricots and put them in a small pan with the wine. Bring to the boil and simmer for 2 or 3 minutes.

2   Season the lamb chops with pepper and cumin. Finely grate the zest from the lemon and squeeze its juice. Crush the garlic. Drain the apricots and reserve the wine.

3   Heat the oil in a large frying pan over a moderate heat. Crush in the garlic and add the lemon zest. Snip in the spring onions and apricots.

4   Sauté for 2 or 3 minutes, stirring frequently.

5   Turn up the heat slightly and cook the lamb chops for 3–5 minutes on each side, depending on how well you wish them to be cooked.

6   Transfer the lamb to a warmed serving dish and keep warm.

7   Deglaze the pan with the honey, lemon juice and reserved wine. Stir and boil for a minute or two to reduce to a coating consistency. Adjust seasoning and pour this sauce over the lamb to serve.

NOISETTES in an ALMOND and LEMON CRUST

● *under 15 minutes*

This treatment works equally well with grilled noisettes and grilled or fried lamb chops.

½ organic uncoated lemon
2 tbsp olive oil
85 g / 3 oz flaked almonds
pinch of ground mace
8 small lamb noisettes, each weighing about
    55–75 g / 2–2½ oz
25 g / ½ oz butter
salt and pepper

1   Halve the lemon half and chop one quarter coarsely. Squeeze the juice from the other piece.

2   In the food processor, whizz to a paste the chopped lemon with half the oil, two-thirds of the almonds, the mace and seasoning to taste. Spread the noisettes with this mixture.

3   Heat the remaining oil in a large frying pan over a moderate to high heat and cook the noisettes in it for 3–5 minutes on each side, depending on how well done you wish the lamb to be.

4   After the noisettes have been carefully turned, add the butter with the remaining almonds to the pan and sauté them as the lamb continues to cook, stirring them frequently.

5   Put the cooked noisettes on warmed plates. Deglaze the pan with the lemon juice and adjust the seasoning if necessary. Pour the sautéed almonds and pan juices over the lamb to serve.

PAN-FRIED LAMB CHOPS with BABY VEGETABLES

🕐 *under 20 minutes*

8 small lamb chops
225 g / 8 oz ripe tomatoes
1 garlic clove
1 little gem lettuce
2 tbsp oil
2 spring onions
115 g / 4 oz baby carrots
115 g / 4 oz French beans
115 g / 4 oz frozen small garden peas
pinch of sugar
salt and pepper

1 Season the lamb chops with pepper. Chop the tomatoes, crush the garlic and shred the lettuce.

2 Heat the oil in a large frying pan over a moderate heat. Snip in the spring onions and add the garlic. Cook for 1 or 2 minutes, stirring frequently.

3 Increase the heat slightly and add the lamb chops. Cook for 3–5 minutes on each side, depending on how well done you wish the lamb to be.

4 Transfer the lamb to a serving dish and keep warm.

5 Lower the heat to moderate. Add the carrots to the pan and sauté them for 2 or 3 minutes.

6 Add the French beans and sauté for a minute or two more. Add the tomatoes, lettuce and peas with a pinch of sugar, cover and simmer for 2 or 3 minutes.

7 Adjust the seasoning, if necessary, and pour over the lamb to serve.

PORK and GAMMON

Pork must be thoroughly cooked through, but it is quite easy to overcook it so that it becomes tough and dry. Cooking it in a tightly covered pan helps the meat retain its succulence. Buy ready trimmed pork chops and flatten them slightly with a mallet or rolling pin to speed cooking. Slash the fat around the edges at 2.5 cm / 1 in intervals to prevent them curling up during cooking.

GAMMON STEAKS with DEVILLED CUMBERLAND SAUCE

🕐 *under 20 minutes*

4 gammon steaks, each about 1–2 cm / $\frac{1}{2}$ – $\frac{3}{4}$ in thick
$\frac{1}{2}$ organic uncoated orange
wedge of organic uncoated lemon
2 shallots
170 g / 6 oz redcurrant jelly
2 tbsp port
1 tsp arrowroot
1 tsp Worcestershire sauce
1 tsp English mustard powder
1 tsp red wine vinegar
pinch of cayenne
2 tbsp oil
salt and pepper

1 Season the gammon steaks with pepper.

2 Pare off several strips of zest from the orange and lemon. Coarsely chop the shallots. Whizz them in the food processor with the pared zest until puréed. Squeeze in the juice from the orange and lemon and add all the remaining ingredients except the oil. Whizz again until well mixed.

3 Heat the oil in a large frying pan over a moderate heat and add the sauce mixture. Sauté for 2 or 3 minutes, stirring frequently.

4 Remove all but 2 tablespoons of the liquid from the pan and keep warm. Increase the heat slightly and add the gammon steaks. Cook for about 4 minutes on each side.

5 Return the rest of the sauce to the pan, cover and simmer gently for about 3–5 minutes. Adjust the seasoning, if necessary, to serve.

Variation:
'Devil' a ready-made Cumberland sauce by simply adding the Worcestershire sauce, mustard, vinegar and cayenne.

'WILD' PORK CHOPS with BEER and JUNIPER BERRIES

🕐 *under 25 minutes*

8 juniper berries
2 garlic cloves
pinch of dried thyme
2 tbsp oil
4 thin pork loin chops
170 g/6 oz ripe tomatoes
2 spring onions
100 ml/$3\frac{1}{2}$ fl oz light beer
salt and pepper

1 In the food processor, whizz the juniper berries with one of the garlic cloves, the thyme, some pepper and half the oil. Spread the chops with this mixture. Coarsely chop the tomatoes and crush the other garlic clove.

2 Heat the remaining oil in a frying pan over a high heat and brown the chops for 3 or 4 minutes on each side. Transfer them to a warmed dish and keep warm.

3 Reduce the heat to moderate and snip in the spring onions. Add the remaining garlic and the tomatoes with any remaining juniper berry mixture. Sauté for 2 or 3 minutes, stirring frequently.

4 Add the beer and boil for a minute or two.

5 Return the chops to the pan, cover and leave to simmer gently for about 7 minutes. Adjust the seasoning to serve.

Variation:
Shred some cabbage into this dish after the chops have been returned to the pan.

PORK CHOPS with APPLE and CALVADOS SAUCE

🕐 *under 25 minutes*

If the chops are really small, you may need 2 per person.

4 thin pork loin chops
3 firm red dessert apples
3 spring onions
1 garlic clove
2 tbsp oil
2 tbsp apple juice
2 tbsp calvados
salt and pepper

1 Season the pork chops. Halve and core the apples. Coarsely chop 2 of them and cut the third into thick slices.

2 Put the chopped apples in the food processor, snip in the spring onions and add the garlic. Pour in half the oil and the apple juice. Season with salt and pepper and whizz until well blended.

3 In a large frying pan, heat the remaining oil over a moderate heat. Add the apple mixture and sliced apples and sauté for 1 or 2 minutes, stirring frequently.

4 Remove all but about 2 tablespoons of the mixture from the pan, turn up the heat slightly and add the chops. Cover and cook for about 10–12 minutes, turning the chops halfway through, until the juices run quite clear when they are pierced.

5 Return the remaining mixture to the pan and add the calvados. Simmer gently for 1 or 2 minutes and adjust the seasoning, if necessary.

Pork Chops with Apple and Calvados Sauce

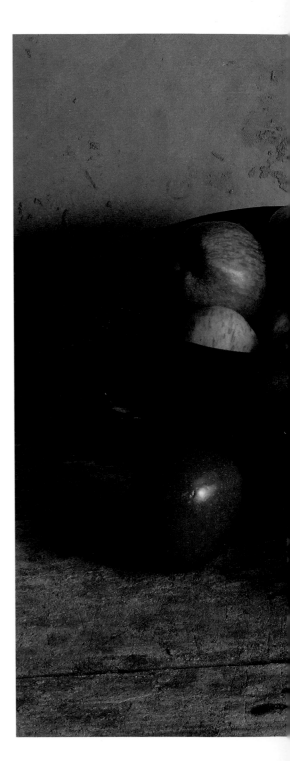

5

VEGETABLES
and SALADS

When cooking in a hurry there is little time to devote to fussy accompaniments. Moreover, good fresh vegetables require the minimum of cooking to preserve their flavour and texture. For this reason we favour techniques like grilling and stir-frying. We also often cook our vegetables either in combination or along with potatoes, rice or noodles.

We take advantage of the increasing number of quick-cook varieties of rice now available. We are also particularly fond of those types of Chinese noodles which need only to be soaked in hot water to be ready to eat. They come in an interesting variety of flavours and are good stir-fried with flavourings and other vegetables.

Top: Grilled Mediterranean Vegetables (page 73); bottom: Basmati Rice with Pine Nuts and Sultanas (page 68)

BASMATI RICE with PINE NUTS and SULTANAS

🕐 *under 15 minutes*

You can now buy varieties of basmati rice in packets which cook in 10 minutes.

500 ml / 16 fl oz chicken or vegetable stock or water
225 g / 8 oz basmati or other long-grain rice
55 g / 2 oz butter
2 tbsp oil
55 g / 2 oz sultanas
2 or 3 sprigs of fresh coriander
55 g / 2 oz pine nuts
salt and pepper

1   Put the stock or water to heat.

2   Rinse the rice thoroughly in a wire sieve under cold running water. Leave it to drain.

3   Melt the butter with the oil in a large heavy-bottomed saucepan over a moderate heat.

4   Add the rice and sultanas. Stir it well to ensure that all the grains are coated.

5   Pour in the boiling stock or water, along with a generous pinch of salt, stir and bring back to the boil.

6   Cover the pan and simmer gently for 8–10 minutes, until all the stock or water has been absorbed and the rice is tender.

7   Snip over the coriander, stir in the pine nuts and season to taste.

Variations:

1   For extra flavour, sauté 2 or 3 snipped spring onions in the butter and oil before adding the rice and then add a pinch of cinnamon with the sultanas.

2   Alternatively, add 85 g / 3 oz frozen small garden peas with the rice at the beginning of cooking and stir in 55 g / 2 oz roasted shelled cashews at the end.

TWICE-COOKED NOODLES with BABY SWEETCORN

🕐 *under 15 minutes*

3 tbsp olive oil
450 g / 1 lb egg noodles
3 spring onions
6 baby sweetcorn
salt and pepper

1   Put 4.5 l / 8 pt of water in a large pan and put on a high heat. Alternatively, to speed things up, heat half the water in the pan and the rest in a kettle. Add a generous pinch of salt and 1 tablespoon of the oil to the water in the pan.

2   Add the noodles and cook them for 3–4 minutes until just soft but still with some resistance to the bite. Drain well.

3   While the noodles are cooking, heat the remaining oil in a wok over a moderate heat. Snip in the spring onions and sweetcorn. Stir-fry for 2 or 3 minutes.

4   Add the cooked and drained noodles with seasoning to taste and stir-fry for another minute or so.

Variations:

1   To accompany highly flavoured dishes, serve the noodles plainly cooked with 1 tablespoon of oil stirred into them.

2   If you use Chinese cellophane noodles, they need only be soaked in boiling water before stir-frying.

3   Stir-fry the noodles with 55 g / 2 oz snipped mange-tout peas and a snipped deseeded chilli pepper.

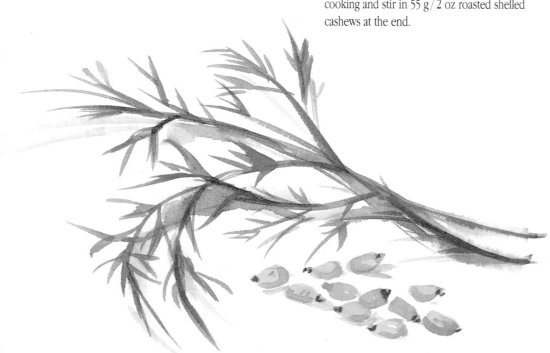

SAUTÉED COURGETTE SHREDS

🕐 *under 10 minutes*

Do not peel the courgettes for this dish. Their size is not important as the shreds cook so quickly, but smaller courgettes will be sweeter.

225 g/8 oz courgettes
55 g/2 oz butter
1 tbsp sunflower oil
salt and pepper

1 Finely shred the courgettes in the food processor, using the grating blade.

2 Melt the butter with the oil in a large sauté pan over a moderate to high heat.

3 Season the butter very generously with salt and pepper.

4 When the pan is very hot, tip in the courgette shreds and stir-fry them briefly until just softened and well coated with the seasoned butter and oil.

Variations:
1 For even more flavour, snip in some tarragon or add some crushed garlic to the pan and cook for a minute or so before adding the courgettes.

2 Sprinkle the shreds with some lemon juice just before serving.

FRENCH BEANS with ANCHOVY BEURRE BLANC SAUCE

🕐 *under 15 minutes*

It is essential to use unsalted butter for this sauce as the anchovies are so salty. To top and tail French beans in a hurry: bang a handful down on one end to align them and then cut those ends off, then repeat with the other end.

450 g/1 lb French beans
3 canned anchovies in oil
2 shallots
150 ml/¼ pt white wine
115 g/4 oz butter
salt and pepper

1 Put a kettle of water to heat. Top and tail the beans.

2 Put the beans in a large pan, cover with boiling water from the kettle and add a generous pinch of salt.

3 Bring to the boil and simmer for 3–5 minutes, until the beans are just tender but still firm to the bite. Drain well.

4 While the beans are cooking, make the sauce: drain and pat the anchovies dry. In the food processor, whizz the shallots and anchovies to a coarse paste.

5 Put this mixture in a small saucepan with the wine, bring to the boil and simmer for a few minutes until syrupy.

6 Off the heat, add the butter in small pieces, whisking them in one at a time until the sauce is smooth and shiny. Season with pepper.

7 Toss the drained beans in the sauce to serve.

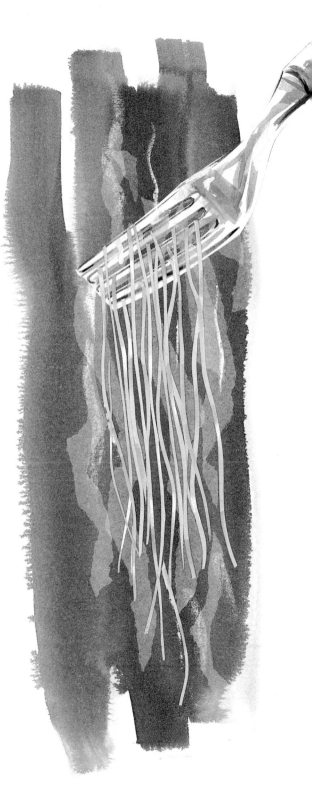

STIR-FRIED LEEKS with JUNIPER BERRIES

under 20 minutes

This dish goes well with grilled meat. Try to use baby leeks if possible. Older leeks will have to be simmered for longer.

6 leeks
1 tbsp juniper berries
1 garlic clove
55 g / 2 oz butter
1 tbsp olive oil
2 tbsp white wine
1 tbsp lemon juice
salt and pepper

1　Trim the leeks and halve them. Wash the grit out carefully under cold running water. Pat the leeks dry and snip them into fine slices. Lightly crush the juniper berries and the garlic clove.

2　Melt the butter with the oil in a sauté pan over a moderate heat and add the juniper berries and garlic. Stir-fry for a minute or so.

3　Add the leeks and stir-fry for 2 or 3 minutes.

4　Add the white wine and lemon juice. Cover the pan and leave to simmer gently for about 3 minutes.

5　Season well with salt and pepper.

Variation:
Stir in 3 or 4 tablespoons of cream and a small pinch of nutmeg to serve with poultry or eggs.

BUTTERED BABY CARROTS with VERMOUTH

under 15 minutes

You can use older carrots, provided they are scraped and sliced and cooked for a few minutes longer.

450 g / 1 lb baby carrots
55 g / 2 oz butter
2 tbsp sweet vermouth
salt and pepper

1　Put the carrots in a large pan and add just enough water to cover. Add a generous pinch of salt and bring to the boil over a high heat.

2　Lower the heat and simmer gently for 4–6 minutes until the carrots are just tender but still firm. Drain well.

3　Return the carrots to the rinsed-out pan and add the butter and vermouth. Season well with salt and pepper.

4　Toss the contents of the pan over a high heat until the carrots are evenly coated with the mixture and have browned slightly.

Left: Stir-fried Leeks with Juniper Berries; right: Buttered Baby Carrots with Vermouth

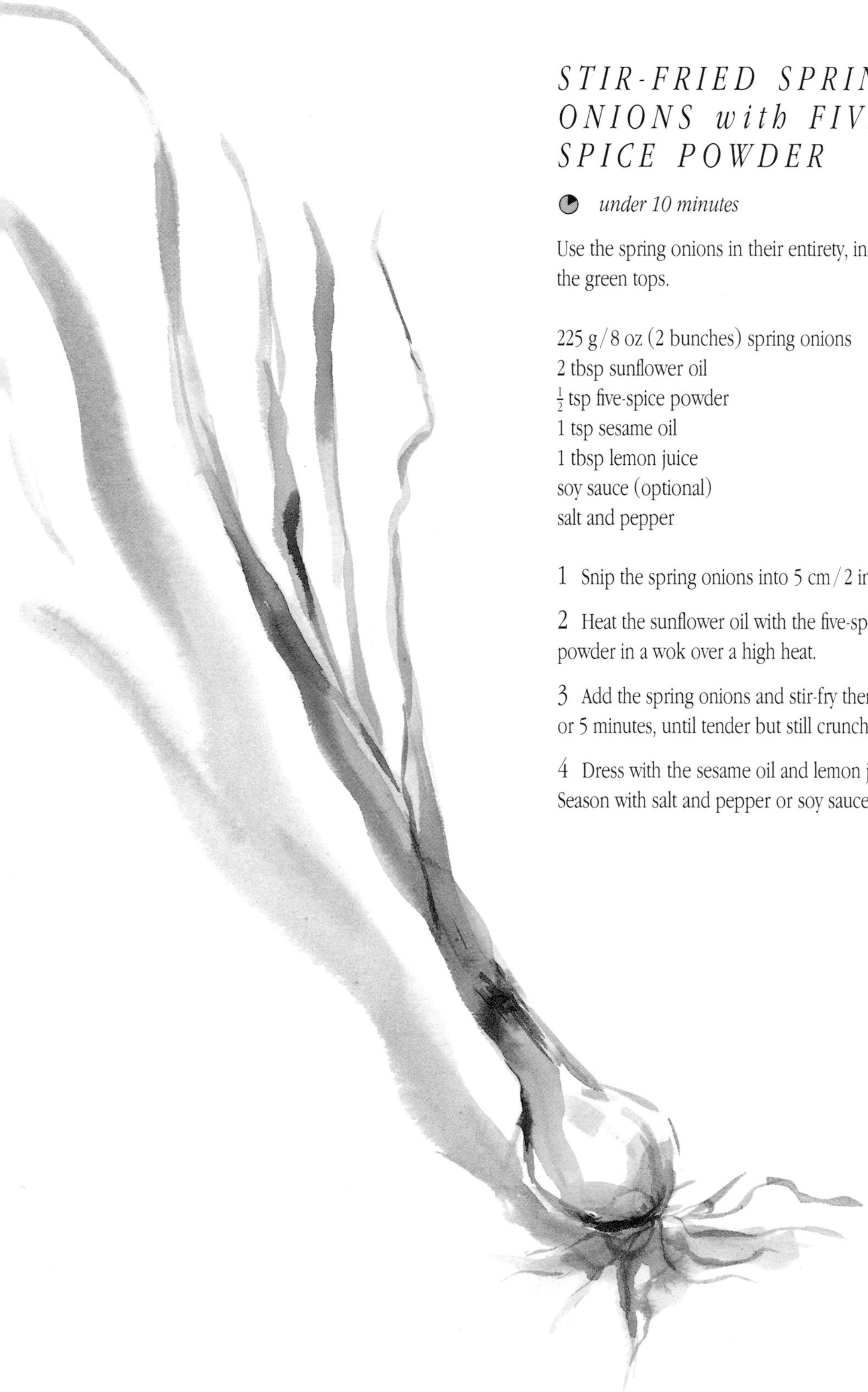

STIR-FRIED SPRING ONIONS *with* FIVE-SPICE POWDER

🕐 *under 10 minutes*

Use the spring onions in their entirety, including the green tops.

225 g / 8 oz (2 bunches) spring onions
2 tbsp sunflower oil
$\frac{1}{2}$ tsp five-spice powder
1 tsp sesame oil
1 tbsp lemon juice
soy sauce (optional)
salt and pepper

1 Snip the spring onions into 5 cm / 2 in lengths.

2 Heat the sunflower oil with the five-spice powder in a wok over a high heat.

3 Add the spring onions and stir-fry them for 4 or 5 minutes, until tender but still crunchy.

4 Dress with the sesame oil and lemon juice. Season with salt and pepper or soy sauce to serve.

BABY NEW POTATOES *with* FRESH HERBS

🕐 *under 15 minutes*

Buy ready scrubbed new potatoes to save time. The smaller they are the faster they cook and if you can't get really small ones, cut them in half. Use any of the suggested herbs, either on their own or in combination.

450 g / 1 lb baby new potatoes
55 g / 2 oz butter
4 or 5 sprigs of fresh herbs, such as chives,
    parsley, mint or basil
salt and pepper

1 Put a kettle of water to heat. Scrub the potatoes but do not peel them.

2 Put the potatoes in a large pan, pour over the boiling water and add a generous pinch of salt. Bring the water back to the boil, reduce the heat and simmer for 4–6 minutes, until the potatoes are just tender but still firm. Drain well.

3 Return the potatoes to the rinsed-out pan, add the butter and snip in the herbs. Season well with salt and pepper.

4 Toss the potatoes over a high heat until they are all well coated with the herbs and butter.

Variations:
1 Dress the cooked potatoes with some Orange and Lemon Butter as described on page 51.

2 Instead of butter, stir in 150 ml / $\frac{1}{4}$ pt of Greek yoghurt, crème fraîche or sour cream and snip in some dill leaves. This dish also works very well cold for buffets or picnics.

GRILLED MEDITERRANEAN VEGETABLES

under 15 minutes

2 small fennel bulbs
2 red sweet peppers
2 yellow sweet peppers
4 baby courgettes
2 red onions
4 plum tomatoes
4 tbsp olive oil
salt

1 Heat a hot grill.

2 Cut the vegetables in half lengthwise. Take out the woody core from the fennel bulbs. Remove the seeds and pith from the peppers.

3 Put the vegetables on the grill rack and brush them well with oil. Sprinkle with coarse salt.

4 Grill the vegetables, turning as necessary and basting with more oil, for about 6–10 minutes, until they are well browned all over.

Variations:
1 Use oil flavoured with herbs, spices or chillis.

2 Snip some fresh oregano or thyme over the vegetables.

PEAS with LETTUCE and SPRING ONIONS

under 10 minutes

Better quality frozen small garden peas are picked and processed so rapidly that they are more sweet, tender and flavourful than all but the peas from your own garden. Use them straight from the packet and don't bother defrosting them first.

55 g / 2 oz butter
2 little gem lettuces
4 spring onions
1 or 2 sprigs of summer savory
350 g / 12 oz frozen small garden peas
pinch of sugar
salt and pepper

1 Melt the butter in a heavy-bottomed pan over a moderate heat.

2 Shred the lettuces coarsely into the bottom of a saucepan. Snip in the spring onions and herbs. Add the peas with the sugar, about 2 tablespoons of water and salt and pepper to taste.

3 Cover the pan tightly, bring to the boil and then simmer very gently for about 5–7 minutes, depending on the size of the peas, until just tender. Shake the pan once or twice during cooking.

Variations:
1 Use thyme or mint instead of the savory.

2 Instead of using butter, first snip 2 slices of streaky bacon into the pan and dry fry them until crisp, then add the other ingredients.

SALADS

More than just the quickest and most satisfying form of vegetable accompaniment, salads can make exciting first courses, healthy snack meals and substantial main courses.

Our approach to making a good salad is simple: freshness and variety are all. Choose from our checklists of good ingredients to make new and interesting combinations every time. We have arranged them so that those ingredients which broadly line up across the page will marry well to give a good salad. Whatever your mix, however, as long as you ensure a good balance of colours, textures and tastes the results will be rewarding.

Make the most of the packets of ready-washed and trimmed leaves, spring onions etc, and your salads will be ready in a matter of minutes. If preparing your own ingredients, make sure that you dry everything thoroughly, preferably in a salad spinner for ease and speed, and simply tear leaves with your hands.

For big mixed salads, use as large a bowl as possible so that you have ample room for tossing and mixing. A big shallow bowl is best as this makes it easier to ensure everyone gets a fair share of all the ingredients.

BASIC LEAVES	FRESH HERBS	VEGETABLES
butterhead lettuce	dill	cucumber, cut into julienne chunks
cos lettuce	parsley	bulb fennel, cored and coarsely chopped
chicory	thyme	sweet peppers, deseeded and snipped into thin strips
iceberg lettuce	chives	celery, trimmed and sliced
Batavian endive	salad burnet	carrots, sliced or cut into julienne chunks
lamb's lettuce	tarragon	cabbage, shredded
curly endive	sweet cicely	Chinese cabbage, sliced or shredded
oakleaf lettuce	chervil	mange-tout peas, trimmed and blanched for 1 or 2 minutes and then snipped into pieces
little gem lettuce	marjoram	cherry tomatoes
treviso	mint	broccoli, separated into florets and blanched for 2 or 3 minutes
lollo rosso	basil	sugar peas, trimmed and blanched for 1 or 2 minutes and then snipped into pieces
radicchio	summer savory	
rocket	sage	French beans, trimmed and blanched for 3 or 4 minutes and then snipped into short lengths
dandelion leaves	fennel	baby sweetcorn, blanched for 1 or 2 minutes and snipped into chunks
watercress	coriander	
baby spinach	borage	leeks, rinsed, blanched for 2 or 3 minutes and sliced into short lengths
sorrel	hyssop	mushrooms, halved or thickly sliced
purslane	oregano	radishes, halved or sliced

BITS AND PIECES

walnuts, whole or coarsely chopped

pistachios, lightly grilled and salted

melon, deseeded and scooped into balls or chopped into cubes

oranges, peeled and thinly sliced

sunflower seeds, dry-fried for 2 or 3 minutes and lightly salted

Parmesan, grated or pared in thin flakes

sesame seeds, dry-fried for 1 or 2 minutes

strawberries, whole, halved or quartered and sprinkled with black pepper

dill and fennel seeds, seasoned with salt and lemon juice

apples, cored and coarsely chopped or sliced

pine nuts, raw or sautéed in oil

hazelnuts, grilled or fried in butter and lightly salted

blue cheese, especially Roquefort, Stilton or Gorgonzola, crumbled

avocados, peeled, stoned and chopped and sprinkled with lemon or lime juice

croutons, fried in a little oil and butter in a pan smeared with garlic

poppy seeds, dry-fried for 1 or 2 minutes

black olives, stoned and chopped or whole

corn chips, crumbled

flaked almonds, grilled or fried in oil until golden and lightly salted

DRESSINGS

Basic Vinaigrette

Tomato and Tarragon Vinaigrette

Horseradish Mayonnaise

Lemon Vinaigrette

Garlic Vinaigrette

Mustard Mayonnaise

Soy and Honey Vinaigrette

Herb Vinaigrette

Balsamic Vinaigrette

Avocado and Sour Cream Vinaigrette

Walnut Oil Vinaigrette

Herb Mayonnaise

Basic Mayonnaise

Aïoli

Harissa and Black Olive Vinaigrette

Blue Cheese Mayonnaise

Orange Mayonnaise

Salsa Verde

Yoghurt and Mint Mayonnaise

SALAD DRESSINGS

The simplest and quickest dressing for salads is a liberal dribbling of very good quality extra-virgin olive oil followed by a sprinkling of sea salt and pepper. However, a wide range of interestingly flavoured vinaigrettes are quite easily made. The salad should be tossed lightly to ensure that all the ingredients are coated with the dressing. Mayonnaise dressings are normally treated more like sauces and served separately or spooned over salads, rather than attempting to coat ingredients with them.

BASIC VINAIGRETTE

🕐 *under 5 minutes*

5 tbsp olive oil
1 tbsp white wine vinegar
1 tsp mustard
salt and pepper

1 In a small bowl or cup, mix the oil and vinegar with the mustard until smooth.

2 Season to taste with pepper and just enough salt for the vinaigrette to stop tasting oily. Mix well again just before pouring over the salad.

Variations:
Lemon Vinaigrette: use lemon juice instead of vinegar.

Balsamic Vinaigrette: use balsamic vinegar.

Garlic Vinaigrette: crush 1 garlic clove into *Basic Vinaigrette.*

Herb Vinaigrette: use lemon juice and snip in some parsley, chives, coriander, basil or fresh thyme.

Tomato and Tarragon Vinaigrette: whizz 225 g / 8 oz ripe tomatoes with a small pinch of sugar, 1 garlic clove and $\frac{1}{2}$ tsp grainy mustard. Snip in some tarragon and mix into a *Basic Vinaigrette* made with red wine vinegar.

Avocado and Sour Cream Vinaigrette: whizz flesh of 1 small avocado with 1 garlic clove and 2 tablespoons of sour cream, mix into *Lemon Vinaigrette.*

Soy and Honey Vinaigrette: use soy sauce instead of vinegar and stir in 1 tablespoon of honey.

Walnut Oil Vinaigrette: use equal parts walnut oil and sunflower oil.

Harissa and Black Olive Vinaigrette: whizz 1 tablespoon of harissa and 3 or 4 stoned black olives and mix this into the *Basic Vinaigrette.*

BASIC MAYONNAISE

🕐 *under 10 minutes*

Make sure all the ingredients are at room temperature to help the emulsion form readily. As the egg is not cooked it is essential that it comes from an impeccable source. Once made, store mayonnaise in the refrigerator.

1 egg
$\frac{1}{2}$ lemon
150 ml / $\frac{1}{4}$ pt olive oil
150 ml / $\frac{1}{4}$ pt sunflower oil
salt and pepper

1 Break the egg into the food processor. Add 1 tablespoon of juice from the lemon and one-quarter of the mixed oils.

2 Whizz briefly. With the machine still running, pour in the remaining oil in a steady stream and process until thick and smooth.

3 Season with salt and pepper and a little more lemon juice, if necessary.

Variations:

Mustard Mayonnaise: add 1 or 2 teaspoons of smooth or grainy mustard to *Basic Mayonnaise*.

Blue Cheese Mayonnaise: whizz 85 g / 3 oz blue cheese with 3 tablespoons of crème fraîche or sour cream, 2 tablespoons of olive oil and 1 tablespoon of lemon juice. Season to taste with pepper.

Aïoli: whizz 3 garlic cloves with 1 egg yolk and then pour in the oils as above. Season to taste with salt, pepper and lemon juice.

Orange Mayonnaise: use orange juice instead of lemon juice.

Yoghurt and Mint Mayonnaise: add 2 tablespoons of Greek yoghurt to *Basic Mayonnaise* and snip in a few fresh mint leaves.

Herb Mayonnaise: snip some herbs into *Basic Mayonnaise*, as for *Herb Vinaigrette*.

Salsa Verde: whizz about 55 g / 2 oz flat-leaf parsley with 2 whole eggs, 4 garlic cloves and 4 drained anchovy fillets; pour in the oils as above; season with pepper and lemon juice.

Horseradish Mayonnaise: flavour *Basic Mayonnaise* with 1 tablespoon creamed horseradish.

MAIN·COURSE SALADS

It is an easy matter to boost a simple salad into a satisfying main course. The addition of some cooked potatoes, flageolets, haricots or chick peas will give substance and crunch, while nuts or chopped boiled eggs can add necessary protein.

For those for whom a main course must contain meat, try arranging some Strips (see pages 46–9) on a bed of lightly dressed mixed leaves. Alternatively shred some smoked fish or chicken or cold roast chicken, or roll slices of cold meats into cylinders and snip them into strips.

SEAFOOD, ASPARAGUS and BROAD BEAN SALAD

◕ *under 15 minutes*

1 small lemon
400 g/14 oz frozen broad beans
12–15 asparagus tips
1 garlic clove
4 tbsp olive oil
3–4 spring onions
225 g/8 oz large cooked prawns or cooked seafood mixture
115 g/4 oz prepared mixed salad leaves
small bunch of chervil
salt and pepper

1 Put some water to heat in the kettle. Squeeze the juice from the lemon.

2 Put the beans and the asparagus in a sauté pan, sprinkle with a little salt and cover with the boiling water. Simmer gently until just tender. Drain well.

3 Rub the rinsed-out and dried sauté pan with the halved garlic clove, add 1 tablespoon of the oil and snip in the spring onions. Sauté for a minute or two and then add the prawns or seafood along with another 1 tablespoon of oil. Sauté for 1 minute only.

4 Meanwhile, shred the salad leaves into a bowl and add 1 tablespoon of oil along with half the lemon juice. Season well with salt and pepper. Toss well to ensure that all the leaves are coated.

5 Pile the prawn or seafood mixture on top of the salad, arrange the asparagus tips on top of that and snip over the chervil. Season again lightly and dribble over the remaining oil and lemon juice.

SPICY AVOCADO and KIDNEY BEAN SALAD

◕ *under 15 minutes*

225 g/8 oz of broccoli florets or 1 large head of broccoli
225 g/8 oz mange-tout peas
1 can (400 g/14 oz) red kidney beans
115 g/4 oz prepared mixed salad leaves
whites of 3 fat spring onions
1 large ripe avocado
$\frac{1}{4}$ lemon
55 g/2 oz black olives
55 g/2 oz croutons
for the dressing:
1 tsp chilli paste or harissa
4 tbsp olive oil
2 tbsp mayonnaise
1 tbsp single cream
2–3 tbsp orange juice
salt and pepper

1 Put some water to heat in the kettle.

2 Cut or shred the broccoli into tiny florets and put them in a saucepan. Sprinkle with a little salt and cover with the boiling water. Simmer for 2 minutes and then add the mange-tout. Simmer for one more minute and then drain well.

3 Meanwhile, drain the beans, shred the salad leaves into a large shallow bowl and thinly slice the spring onions. Halve, peel and stone the avocado. Chop the flesh and squeeze lemon juice over it.

4 Combine the dressing ingredients well in a small bowl or jug with salt and pepper to taste.

5 Pour a little of the dressing over the leaves and toss them well. Toss in the beans and sliced spring onions along with a little more of the dressing.

6 Add the olives, croutons, mange-tout and broccoli and toss with a little more of the dressing. Add the avocado and remaining dressing.

WATERCRESS, BEETROOT and HOT POTATO SALAD

◕ *under 15 minutes*

450 g/1 lb baby new potatoes
115 g/4 oz prepared watercress
2 little gem lettuces
4 spring onions
2 heads of chicory
2 cooked and peeled beetroot
for the dressing:
3 tbsp Dijon mustard
5 tbsp olive oil
small bunch of parsley
small bunch of chives
salt and pepper

1 Put some water to heat in the kettle.

2 Halve the potatoes, or cut them into quarters if large, and put them in a pan. Add some salt and cover with the boiling water. Simmer until just tender, but still very firm. Drain well.

3 Meanwhile, shred the watercress and lettuce leaves into a salad bowl and snip over the spring onion. Remove the hard core from the chicory heads and snip them into the salad. Dice the beetroot into a small bowl.

4 Make the dressing: put the mustard into a bowl and gradually pour in the oil, stirring continuously, as if making mayonnaise. When the oil has all been incorporated, snip in the herbs and season to taste with salt and pepper.

5 When the potatoes are cooked, drain them well and add them to the salad. Pour over the dressing and sprinkle in the beetroot. Mix well to ensure that all the ingredients are coated in the sauce.

Spicy Avocado and Kidney Bean Salad

Variations:

1 Dry-fry 3 or 4 slices of bacon and snip them in with the potatoes. You can also deglaze the pan with a little white wine vinegar and add that to the salad for extra flavour.

2 Hard-boil some eggs in the potato water and chop them into the salad. Use some of the egg yolk mashed in with the mustard to give extra body to the sauce.

6

LAST COURSES

When there is no time to bake cakes, tarts or soufflés, fruit is the salvation of the quick cook. Most good ripe seasonal fruit is so full of natural flavour that very little help is needed to bring it out. We marinate fruit briefly in flavoured alcohol, skewer exciting combinations of fruit on kebabs and grill them lightly, wrap them in parcels and bake them for a few minutes or purée with cream into fools.

Our other great ally is good vanilla ice-cream which we recommend that you always keep in the freezer to serve with one of our five-minute sauces.

Various Fruit Kebabs (pages 84–5)

MARINATED FRUIT

Prepare the fruit before the meal and leave to marinate, preferably in the refrigerator, stirring occasionally when you get the chance between courses. Serve with bowls of crème fraîche or Greek yoghurt, which may also be flavoured with finely grated lemon, orange or grapefruit zest. Garnish with a few tiny mint leaves or sprigs of lemon balm.

STRAWBERRIES in RASPBERRY VINEGAR with BLACK PEPPER

under 15 minutes

If in a real hurry, don't bother to hull the strawberries, just wipe them with a damp cloth.

450 g / 1 lb strawberries
coarsely ground black pepper
1 tsp icing sugar
3 tbsp raspberry vinegar

1 Hull and wash the strawberries. Pat them dry. Cut any large ones in half.

2 Place them in a serving bowl and sprinkle generously with coarsely ground black pepper. Sprinkle over the sugar and the vinegar. Mix carefully.

3 Chill for at least 10 minutes.

CHERRIES IN EAU-DE-VIE

under 15 minutes

450 g / 1 lb ripe sweet cherries
3 tbsp kirsch or brandy
1 tbsp soft brown sugar

1 Remove the stalks from the cherries, wash them and pat them dry.

2 Put them in a serving bowl and sprinkle over the alcohol and the sugar.

3 Chill for at least 10 minutes.

PEACHES in SPARKLING WHITE WINE

under 15 minutes

Use yellow peaches which are ripe but not too soft to handle.

4 large ripe peaches
1 tbsp Cognac
$\frac{1}{2}$ bottle (350 ml / 12 fl oz) well chilled dry or semi-sweet sparkling white wine

1 Wash the peaches and pat them dry. Cut them in half and remove the stones. Slice the halves again into quarters and then slice these again in two.

2 Put the peaches in bowls or pile them in tall glasses, add a dash of Cognac to each and pour in enough wine to cover.

3 Chill for at least 10 minutes.

Variation:
Use the more delicately flavoured white peaches, when available, but omit the Cognac.

Clockwise from left: Strawberries in Raspberry Vinegar with Black Pepper, Cherries in Eau-de-vie and Peaches in Sparkling White Wine

FRUIT KEBABS

Most firm fruit grills well in a matter of minutes. Cut pears, apples and fresh pineapples in thick slices or chunks, quarter citrus fruits, halve apricots and plums, and leave strawberries and grapes whole. Make the kebabs up before the meal and sprinkle any cut fruit with lemon juice to keep them from discolouring.

A wide variety of sweet butter sauces may be made to dress the kebabs by whizzing soft unsalted butter with any number of flavourings. Among the best are ginger, brown sugar or honey, spirits, such as rum, gin or whisky, or liqueurs, such as Cointreau or Amaretto.

Always collect precious pan juices and spoon them over the kebabs.

PEAR, GRAPE and CAPE GOOSEBERRY KEBABS

🕐   *under 10 minutes*

Orange and Lemon Butter (see page 51)
4 ripe but firm pears
4 cape gooseberries
about 12 large seedless black grapes
about 12 large seedless green grapes

1 Heat the grill until hot. Put the butter in a warm place to soften it.

2 Halve the pears and remove their cores. Halve the cape gooseberries.

3 Thread the fruit alternately on 4 wooden skewers, starting and finishing with a halved cape gooseberry.

4 Brush all the fruit with some of the softened butter and grill for 1 minute on each side.

5 Serve with the remaining butter dotted or trickled over them.

FIG and GRAPEFRUIT KEBABS with MAPLE SYRUP BUTTER

🕐   *under 10 minutes*

The maple syrup butter goes well with many types of fruit, especially sharp ones.

4 fresh figs
2 small pink grapefruit
2 tbsp flaked almonds
for the maple syrup butter:
55 g / 2 oz unsalted butter, softened
2 tbsp maple syrup

1 Heat the grill until hot.

2 Cut the figs in half lengthwise, or quarters if large. Peel the grapefruit and divide into segments.

3 Cut the butter into pieces and put in the food processor. Whizz with the maple syrup until smooth.

4 Arrange alternating pieces of different fruit on 8 small skewers and brush them with a little of the maple syrup butter.

5 Sprinkle them with some of the almonds. Mix the remaining almonds with the remaining butter and spread around the grill pan.

6 Grill the kebabs for 1 minute on each side, stirring the almonds in the pan from time to time so that they toast evenly.

7 Sprinkle the toasted almonds over the kebabs to serve.

STRAWBERRY and NECTARINE KEBABS with BRANDY BUTTER

under 10 minutes

½ lemon
24 strawberries
2 ripe but firm nectarines
for the brandy butter:
55 g / 2 oz unsalted butter, softened
1 tbsp soft brown sugar
2 tbsp brandy

1   Heat the grill until hot.

2   Squeeze the juice from the lemon, cut the nectarines into halves, remove the stones and cut them again into quarters. Brush them lightly with the lemon juice.

3   Cut the butter into pieces and put in the food processor. Add the sugar and brandy and whizz until smooth.

4   Thread alternating pieces of different fruit on 8 small skewers and brush them with a little of the brandy butter.

5   Grill the kebabs for 1 minute on each side and serve dotted with any remaining brandy butter.

Variation:
Use plums and apricots.

 ## FRUIT GRATINS

Any number of fruits suit this treatment. Have the dish ready to go under the grill as soon as the main course is over, but sprinkle on the sugar only at the last minute.

APRICOT GRATIN with CHOCOLATE SHAVINGS

under 15 minutes

8 ripe apricots
85 g / 3 oz dark chocolate
100 ml / 3 ½ fl oz Greek yoghurt
3 tbsp granulated sugar

1   Heat a hot grill.

2   Halve and stone the apricots. Pull a knife across the chocolate to curl it up in thin strips.

3   Arrange the apricot halves in a gratin dish, hollows up, spoon the yoghurt over the top and sprinkle with the sugar.

4   Grill until the sugar caramelizes.

5   Dot the top with the chocolate shavings.

Variation:
For an even more adventurous dish, spoon a little marmalade over the apricots and sprinkle with a little orange liqueur.

MANGO and PINEAPPLE GRATIN with RUM

under 15 minutes

1 large ripe mango
1 large fresh pineapple
2 tbsp rum
100 ml / 3½ fl oz double cream
3 tbsp soft brown sugar

1   Heat the grill.

2   Peel the mango and slice the flesh. Peel, core and slice the pineapple into chunks.

3   Arrange the fruit in a gratin dish or 4 flameproof ramekins and sprinkle over the rum.

4   Pour the cream over the top and sprinkle with the sugar.

5   Grill until the sugar caramelizes.

Variations:
1   A small pinch of freshly grated nutmeg and 1 or 2 tablespoons of lime juice will give an authentic Caribbean flavour.

2   Try replacing the cream with crème fraîche, Greek yoghurt or mascarpone cheese.

FRUIT PARCELS

Wrapping mixtures of firm fruits in metal foil or greaseproof paper keeps in all their flavours and juices. They can be baked while the meal is in progress. Open the parcels slightly as they are served to allow the aromas to waft up.

BANANA and CHOCOLATE PARCELS

🕐 *under 15 minutes*

4 ripe bananas
55 g / 2 oz unsalted butter
225 g / 8 oz dark chocolate

1 Heat the oven to 220C / 425F / gas7.

2 Cut out 4 squares of foil or paper large enough to wrap the bananas generously.

3 Peel the bananas and place them on the squares.

4 Put one-quarter of the butter on each banana and grate the chocolate over the fruit.

5 Wrap up the parcels loosely, folding over edges to seal them well.

6 Bake for 10 minutes.

RED FRUIT, APPLE and KIRSCH PARCELS

🕐 *under 10 minutes*

Use a mixed red fruit jam with a high fruit content.

30 g / 1 oz unsalted butter
4 ripe dessert apples, such as Granny Smiths
1 small punnet of redcurrants
2 tbsp red fruit preserves
2 tbsp kirsch

1 Heat the oven to 220C / 425F / gas7.

2 Cut out 4 squares of foil or paper large enough to wrap the fruit generously and grease them with the butter.

3 Peel, halve and core the apples. Cut the halves into thick slices and arrange them in 4 piles on the squares.

4 Take the stalks off the redcurrants and divide them between the parcels. Spoon on the preserves and sprinkle over the liqueur.

5 Wrap up the parcels loosely, folding over edges to seal them well.

6 Bake for about 10 minutes.

PEAR and BLUE CHEESE PARCELS

🕐 *under 15 minutes*

This is a very good way of combining a fruit and cheese course.

4 ripe but firm pears, preferably Williams
2 sweet digestive biscuits
30 g / 1 oz unsalted butter
170 g / 6 oz good blue cheese, such as Roquefort, Stilton or Gorgonzola
6 tbsp honeyed sweet white wine, such as Beaume-de-Venise

1 Heat the oven to 220C / 425F / gas7.

2 Peel, halve and core the pears. Cut the flesh into thick strips and cut out four large squares of foil or greaseproof paper.

3 On each square pile a sliced pear and then crumble over half a biscuit. Dot with one-quarter of the butter and then crumble over the cheese or cut it in small slices and dot these over the pears. Pour over one-quarter of the wine and then wrap up the parcels loosely, folding over the edges to seal them well.

4 Bake for 10 minutes.

Red Fruit, Apple and Kirsch Parcels

FRUIT FOOLS

Use only really ripe soft fruit. Serve fruit fools accompanied by small dessert biscuits, such as amaretti or langues-de-chat.

NECTARINE and ALMOND FOOL

🕐   *under 5 minutes*

2 tbsp toasted almonds
450 g / 1 lb ripe nectarines
3 tbsp almond liqueur
4 tbsp double cream
about 55 g / 2 oz icing sugar

1 Heat the grill.

2 Scatter the almonds in the grill pan and toast them lightly on both sides.

3 While they are toasting, stone and coarsely chop the nectarines.

4 Whizz the chopped nectarines in the food processor with the almond liqueur.

5 Add the cream and whizz again briefly.

6 Sweeten to taste with icing sugar.

7 Sprinkle with the toasted almonds to serve.

GOOSEBERRY and ELDERFLOWER WINE FOOL

🕐   *under 5 minutes*

Use very ripe dessert gooseberries. The amount of honey may be reduced according to how sweet they are.

675 g / 1½ lb ripe gooseberries
3 tbsp elderflower wine
about 4 tbsp clear honey
4 tbsp double cream

1 Whizz the gooseberries in the food processor.

2 Press them through a sieve.

3 Return them to the food processor and whizz briefly with the elderflower wine and two-thirds of the honey.

4 Add the cream and whizz again briefly to mix.

5 If necessary, stir in more honey to sweeten to taste.

ICE-CREAM SAUCES

Probably the easiest means of providing a quick last course is simply to buy a good quality vanilla ice-cream and serve it with a five-minute home-made sauce.

HOT WHITE CHOCOLATE SAUCE

🕐 *under 5 minutes*

30 g / 1 oz unsalted butter
85 g / 3 oz white chocolate
2 tbsp double cream

1 Melt the butter in a small saucepan over a gentle heat along with 2 tablespoons of water.

2 Break in the chocolate and stir until it has all melted and the mixture is smooth.

3 Stir in the cream.

Variation:
Add 1 tablespoon of kirsch or other white brandy.

PEANUT BUTTER and JELLY SAUCE

🕐 *under 5 minutes*

30 g / 1 oz unsalted butter
4 tbsp smooth peanut butter
4 tbsp red fruit jelly or jam, preferably raspberry

1 Melt the butter in a small pan over a gentle heat.

2 Add the peanut butter, mix well and heat through.

3 Carefully mix in the fruit jam or jelly, but do not blend. It should be streaked through the sauce.

4 Heat through gently before serving.

RAISIN, HONEY and GRAPPA SAUCE

🕐 *under 5 minutes*

3 tbsp clear honey
2 tbsp grappa or other white brandy
85 g / 3 oz seedless raisins

1 Heat the honey with the grappa in a small pan.

2 Stir in the raisins and mix well to ensure that they are all coated.

Variation:
If you have the time, very gently simmer the raisins in the honey with half the liquor for about 10 minutes. Stir in the remaining liquor to serve.

RED FRUIT SAUCE

🕐 *under 5 minutes*

6 tbsp red fruit jam
½ lemon
2 tbsp raspberry or plum brandy

1 Heat the jam in a small pan over a gentle heat.

2 Finely grate the zest and squeeze the juice from the lemon.

3 Stir the lemon zest and juice along with the brandy into the jam.

4 Mix well.

7

MENU
SUGGESTIONS

To help the reader make the most of the recipes in this book we have set out a selection of menus for all occasions. They not only provide the necessary balance of ingredients, tastes and textures but also work well and efficiently in the kitchen.

Although a large number of our menus are conventional three-course meals, many are also built around the increasingly popular practice of making a meal out of two or three smaller dishes. This approach has the advantage of being highly flexible: simple casual lunches or suppers may easily be transformed into formal dinners with the addition of one or two more dishes.

All our menus are strongly themed to help make selection easier, and for those in a really serious hurry our Ultra-quick section provides instant meals for all situations.

Carrots Vinaigrette (page 28)
Grilled steak with Blue Cheese Butter (page 59)
Twice-cooked Noodles with Baby Sweetcorn (page 68)
Nectarine and Almond Fool (page 88)

FAMILY and CASUAL MEALS

Quick Bolognese (*page 42*)
Salad of mixed leaves with Lemon Vinaigrette (*page 76*)
Cheese and seasonal fruit

Quick Poule au Pot with Smoked Ham (*page 54*)
Baby New Potatoes with Fresh Herbs (*page 72*)
Ice-cream with Red Fruit Sauce (*page 89*)

Pork Strips with Pizzaiola Sauce (*page 47*)
Tagliatelle with Poached Baby Vegetables (*page 42*)
Fig and Grapefruit Kebabs with Maple Syrup Butter (*page 85*)

Herby Scrambled Eggs on Muffins (*page 36*)
Cannellini Bean, Garlic and Curly Endive Soup (*page 24*)
Yoghurt with honey

Stir-fried Chicken, Oyster Mushrooms and Spring Onions (*page 55*)
Chinese no-cook noodles
Salad with Chinese cabbage, snipped spring onions and Soy and Honey Vinaigrette (*page 76*)
Fresh fruit

Cream of Mushroom Muffins (*page 34*)
Gammon Steaks with Devilled Cumberland Sauce (*page 63*)
Buttered Baby Carrots with Vermouth (*page 70*)
Plum and Apricot Kebabs (*page 85*)

CHILDREN'S MEALS

Baby Tomato and Pesto Mini Pizzas (*page 32*)
Do-it-yourself salad (*pages 74–5*)
Banana and Chocolate Parcels (*page 86*)

Quick Carbonara (*page 38*)
with added peas and broccoli florets
Ice-cream with Peanut Butter and Jelly Sauce (*page 89*)

Potato Scones with Maple-cure Bacon and Blue Cheese (*page 36*)
Green salad with a poached egg
Fresh fruit

Multicoloured pasta shaped with Leek and Cheddar Sauce (*page 41*)
Fruit kebabs with Maple Syrup Butter (*page 84*)

Beef strips with Blue Cheese Butter (*page 59*)
Spaghettini with Sautéed Courgette Shreds (*page 69*)
Apricot Gratin with Chocolate Shavings (*page 85*)

ULTRA-QUICK

SPEEDY LIGHT LUNCH
Mixed leaf salad with watercress, lamb's lettuce and Stir-fried Spring Onions and Parma Ham Croûtes (*page 36*)
Pear and Blue Cheese Parcels (*page 86*)

MIXED GRILL MENU
Mozzarella, Anchovy and Capers on Toast (*page 32*)
Grilled steak with Mustard Butter (*page 59*)
Mixed salad with Garlic Vinaigrette (*page 76*)
Blue Cheese and biscuits
Mango and Pineapple Gratin with Rum (*page 85*)

QUICK SUMMER LUNCH
Mixed leaf salad with flageolets and Tuna fish, Red Onion and Olive Oil Sauce (*page 43*)
Strawberries in Raspberry Vinegar with Black Pepper (*page 82*)

QUICK PARTY MENU
Gravlax and Crème fraîche on Rye Bread (*page 34*)
Noodles with Prawn, Sugar Peas and Chilli Oil Sauce (*page 41*)
Salad of mixed leaves with chopped avocado, snipped spring onions and Garlic Vinaigrette (*page 76*)
Peaches in Sparkling White Wine (*page 82*)

NO-COOK SUPPER
Cold Cream of Tomato Soup with Chervil (*page 20*)
Bresaola with Shaved Parmesan and Olive Oil (*page 28*)
Salad of mixed leaves with kidney beans, crumbled corn chips and Harissa and Black Olive Vinaigrette (*page 76*)
Cherries in Eau-de-vie (*page 82*) with Greek yogurt

COUCH-POTATO SNACK SUPPER
Pea and Smoked Ham soup (*page 22*) served with Bruschetta with Ciabatta (*page 35*)

TRATTORIA SUPPER
Stir-fried Spring Onion and Parma Ham Croûtes (*page 36*)
Spaghetti with Salami, Parsley and Olive Sauce (*page 38*)
Mixed leaf salad with Balsamic Vinaigrette (*page 76*)
Ice-cream with Raisin, Honey and Grappa Sauce (*page 89*)

VEGETARIAN

LUNCH ON THE RUN
Quick Soupe au Pistou (*page 22*) without the smoked ham
Green salad with Herb Vinaigrette (*page 76*)
Bread and cheese
Fresh fruit

QUICK AND EASY SUPPER
Mini Cauliflowers in Stilton Sauce (*page 30*)
Spicy Avocado and Kidney Bean Salad (*page 78*)
Peaches in Sparkling White Wine (*page 82*)

CASUAL ENTERTAINING
Grilled Mediterranean Vegetables (*page 73*)
Spaghettini with Crushed Nut Vinaigrette (*page 38*)
Cheese
Ice-cream with Red Fruit Sauce (*page 89*)

SUMMER DINNER
Cold Avocado, Spinach and Spring Onion Soup (*page 20*)
Tagliarini with Tomato and Fennel Sauce (*page 40*)
Green salad dressed with a little olive oil
Pear and Blue Cheese Parcels (*page 86*)

COSY DINNER FOR FRIENDS
Cream of Mushroom Muffins (*page 34*)
Watercress, Beetroot and Hot Potato Salad (*page 78*)
Mango and Pineapple Gratin with Rum (*page 85*)

ENTERTAINING

SUMMER'S EVE SUPPER
Cold Cream of Tomato Soup with Chervil (*page 20*)
Pan-fried Trout with Nut Sauce (*page 53*)
Peas with Lettuce and Spring Onions (*page 73*)
Peaches with Sparkling White Wine (*page 82*)

LIGHT SUPPER À LA MODE
Cold Fresh Herb Soup (*page 20*)
King Prawns Sautéed with Ginger and Chilli (*page 31*)
Salad of mixed leaves and Stir-fried Spring Onions with Five-spice Powder (*page 72*)
Strawberries in Raspberry Vinegar with Black Pepper (*page 82*)

EASY BUT IMPRESSIVE
Bresaola with Shaved Parmesan and Olive Oil (*page 28*)
Salmon Steaks with a Light Salsa (*page 53*)
Baby New Potatoes with Fresh Herbs (*page 72*)
French Beans with Anchovy Beurre Blanc Sauce (*page 69*)
Gooseberry and Elderflower Wine Fool (*page 88*)

MEATLESS MENUS
Guacamole on Walnut Bread (*page 34*)
Seafood, Asparagus and Broad Bean Salad (*page 78*)
Selection of English cheeses
Strawberry and Nectarine Kebabs with Brandy Butter (*page 85*)

Papaya with Smoked Mackerel Mousse (*page 30*)
Tagliatelle with Wilted Spinach Leaves and Bacon (*page 41*)
Salad of mixed sharp leaves with pine nuts and Basic Vinaigrette (*page 76*)
Cheese

WINTER SUPPER
Grilled Radicchio with Goats' Cheese (*page 28*)
Pork Chops with Apple and Calvados Sauce (*page 64*)
Stir-fried Leeks with Juniper Berries (*page 70*)
Ice-cream with White Chocolate Sauce (*page 89*)

QUICK SUNDAY LUNCH
Rigatoni with Smoked Salmon, Sour Cream and Chives (*page 40*)
Chicken Drumsticks with Salsa Verde (*page 55*)
Sautéed Courgette Shreds (*page 69*)
Cheese and fresh fruit

DINNER À DEUX
Carrots Vinaigrette (*page 28*)
Grilled Steaks with Olive and Anchovy Butter (*page 58*)
Twice-cooked Noodles with Baby Sweetcorn (*page 68*)
Nectarine and Almond Fool (*page 88*)

INDEX